Reality Check

by Blaine Bartel

Harrison House
Tulsa, Oklahoma

10 09 08 07 06   10 9 8 7 6 5 4 3 2 1

Reality Check
Finding God's Truth in TV's Reality
ISBN 1-57794-801-7
Copyright © 2006 by Blaine Bartel
P. O. Box 691923
Tulsa, Oklahoma 74179

Published by Harrison House, Inc.
P. O. Box 35035
Tulsa, Oklahoma 74153

Compilation of lists and writing and composition of section Introductions by Shawna McMurry in association with Bordon Books, Tulsa, Oklahoma.

Contents

INTRODUCTION: GOD'S REALITY ABOUT YOU ix

Being Yourself: Simon Says 1

5 Roads to Popularity Without Losing
Your Reputation 3

5 Habits of Happy Teens 4

6 Things You Must Believe About Yourself 5

3 Ways to Discover Who You Are 6

3 Reasons Why Cool Doesn't Try—It Is 7

Self-Image: A Model of Confidence 9

5 Signs of a Confident Person 11

4 Differences Between Confidence and Arrogance 12

4 Ways to Discover What You Can Do 13

4 Reasons You Should Be Cool 14

6 Ways Any Person Can Become Cool 15

3 Musts for Building Real Confidence 16

6 Enemies That Will Try to Steal Your Confidence ..17

7 Scriptures That Prove God Is Confident in You 19

Choices: Clean Your Room! 21

5 Decisions Young People Make That Sabotage
Their Future 23

3 Reasons Your Musical Choices Are Important 24

4 Danger Zones in Modern Entertainment...............25

5 Ways to Have a Great Time Without
Compromising 26

5 Scriptures to Guide Your Daily
Entertainment Choices 27

Freedom: Free at Last! 29

2 Things Freedom Is Not 32

2 Mistakes Teenagers Make in a Desire
for Freedom...33

3 Freedoms You Are Entitled to Every Day 34

3 Sacrifices That Will Guarantee Freedom 35

Serving: Can You Really Win by Losing? 37

5 Unselfish Acts in the Bible 39

4 Reasons People Become Selfish............40

4 Qualities of a Great Teammate 41

5 Ways to Lead Without Being a Captain 43

Forgiveness: Who Let the "Dog" Out? 45

4 Steps to Finding Favor With God.........47

7 Things God Did in Loving Us 48

2 Reasons You May Not Feel Forgiven.....................49

3 Ways to Know That You Have Not Committed
the Unpardonable Sin 50

7 Bible Guarantees for Forgiveness 52

GOD'S REALITY ABOUT HIMSELF

Salvation: The Ultimate Makeover 55

3 Things God's Love Does to People.........................57

3 Ways to Lift Jesus Up in Your World 58

5 Keys to Keep Christ First 59

7 Personal Beliefs That Will Alter Your Future 60

3 Daily Habits to Grow in Your Relationship
With God 61

Following God's Plan: An Amazing Journey 63

4 Ways God Gives You Direction 65

7 Absolutes of God's Will for Your Life 66

7 Scriptures to Guide Your Future............67

5 Sources of Reliable Counsel 68

4 Things to Look for in a Mentor............69

4 Steps to Knowing God's Leading 70

7 Bible Guarantees for Direction 72

4 Ways to Discover Your Life's Calling 74

3 Keys to Forecasting the Future 75

Prayer: God Is Watching 77

3 Secrets to Answered Prayer 79

3 Ways to Lift Up a Person Through Prayer 80

5 Scriptures to Pray Over Your Family....................81

4 Scriptures to Pray Over Your Plan 83

Sharing God's Word: Permanent Immunity 85

4 Scriptures That Promise Salvation 87

3 Steps to Lead a Person to Christ...........................88

3 Practical Ways to Show God's Love to a Sinner 89

4 Do's That Affect Sinners....................................90

3 Attitudes That Make You a Hypocrite 91

5 Things You Should Know About Sinners................92

3 Reasons Leadership Creates Evangelism 93

GOD'S REALITY ABOUT OTHERS

Friendship: Real World Friendship 95

6 Keys to Getting Along With a Roommate.............97

5 Surefire Ways to Make New Friends in a
New Place 99

5 Ways to Attract New Friends 101

5 Questions Real Friends Should Ask Each Other ..102

4 Steps to Building Strong Relationships With
the Friends You Already Have 103

4 Steps to Finding Favor With Friends 105

7 Bible Guarantees for Friendship 106

5 Attitudes That Are Friend Magnets 108

4 Ways to Make a Relationship "Win-Win"...........109

3 Secrets to Making New Friends 110

3 Friendship Killers You Must Avoid 111

**Getting Along With Your Parents: Parents Just
Don't Understand** 113

3 Steps to Finding Favor With Your Parents 115

3 Marks of a Proud Parent 116

3 Ways to Deal With Tough Parents 117

4 Ways to Tell Parents "Thank You" 118

3 Reasons to Help Your Parents............................119

3 Ways Helping Your Parents Helps You 120

3 Things You Must Tell Your Parents 121

2 Things Never to Tell Your Parents 122

7 Questions to Ask Your Parents in the Next
7 Days 123

7 Things a Parent Loves in a Teenager 124

3 Reasons Your Relationship With Your Parents
Will Affect Your Career 125

**Helping Friends in Need: Friends Through
Thick and Thin** 127

4 Reasons It's Critical That You Listen to People ..129

3 Secrets of a Good Listener 130

3 Messages That Lift People Up 131

7 Ways to Help a Suicidal Person 132

3 Things to Say to a Victim of Divorce 133

5 Things an Addict Needs to Know 134

GOD'S REALITY ABOUT YOUR FUTURE

Setting and Achieving Goals: God-Made 137

4 Surefire Ways to Discover Your Talents 139

3 Keys to Effective Planning 140

8 Goals to Reach Before You're 18 141

3 Problems of Those Who Don't Plan 142

4 Steps to a Plan That Works 143

6 Keys to Getting the Most Out of Your Time 144

4 Ways to Discover What You Can Do 145

Success at Work: You're Hired! 147

6 Steps to Finding Favor in the Workplace 149

5 Ways to Get a Great Job 150

5 Qualities of a Valuable Employee 151

7 Rewards of a Diligent Worker 152

4 Kinds of People Who Constantly Get Fired..........153

5 Things God Says About Work 154

6 Keys to Being Promoted by Your Boss 155

3 Secrets to Real Success 156

3 Reasons It Is Cool to Make Good Money 157

3 Keys to Discovering Your Career............................158

6 Careers You Can Start in Your Teens 159

3 Reasons to Quit Your Job 160

4 Secrets to Make Work Go Fast 161

5 Qualities of a Job Well Done 162

4 Ways to Get Hard Work Done More Quickly........163

3 Reasons "Working Hard" Levels the
Playing Field..165

4 Bible Verses to Help You Work Better 167

Overcoming Fear: Is Fear a Factor?........................169

4 Fears You Must Conquer Every Day 172

3 Keys to Motivating Yourself to Do
Difficult Things..173

4 Obstacles That Come With Every
Great Opportunity 174

3 Reasons Your Thoughts Will Affect
Your Performance 176

3 Thoughts You Must Keep Out 177

Giving: Extreme Giving 179

4 Reasons You'll Have More by Giving Away 181

3 Reasons You Should Tithe...................................182

7 Rewards of the Giver 183

3 Reasons God Wants You to Be a Channel 184

3 Keys That Will Open the Windows of Heaven......185

7 Promises Guaranteed to Every Giver 186

5 Ways You Can Give Without Using Money..........187

3 Kinds of Giving Every Person Ought to Do..........188

3 Reasons Givers Find Unusual Favor 189

5 Scriptures That Focus on Giving 190

GOD'S REALITY ABOUT LOVE, SEX, AND DATING

Love: Will You Accept This Rose? 193

3 Reasons Friendship Is More Important
Than Romance 196

3 Things Love Is Not 197

6 Attributes of Real Love......................................198

5 Signs a Relationship Is Centered on the Love
of God 199

Dating: Oh, the Drama! 201

3 Steps to Finding Favor With the Opposite Sex 203

3 Things Dating Is Not 204

3 Ways Christian Dating Is Different 205

4 Signs That You May Not Be Ready to Date.........206

4 Reasons Not to Try Too Hard 207

6 Reasons to Break Up With Someone 208

3 Uncommon Things Every Girl Wants in a Guy 209

3 Uncommon Things Every Guy Wants in a Girl 210

Sexual Temptation: Don't Even Go There 213

6 Reasons to Say No to Premarital Sex 215

7 Ways to Avoid Premarital Sex............................216

5 Steps to Overcoming Tough Temptations 217

3 Important Steps to Take If You've
Sinned Sexually....................................219

4 Signs a Relationship Is Lust-Centered 220

4 Ways to Avoid Sexual Temptation.......................222

5 Reasons to Maintain Sexual Purity
Before Marriage 223

Marriage: Before "I Do"...............................225

7 Areas of Preparation You Must Complete
Before You Are Married......................................227

6 Habits You Must Establish Now If You Hope
to Enjoy a Happy Marriage 229

5 Signs That You May Be Ready to Marry.............231

3 Things Marriage Will Do for You 233

3 Things Marriage Won't Do for You 235

4 Habits of a Happy Marriage 237

PERFECT IMMUNITY...................................239

PRAYER FOR PERFECT IMMUNITY 241

Introduction
GOD'S REALITY ABOUT YOU

In today's culture, reality shows abound. Flip through the channels on a given day, and you can find a reality show on almost any topic, from fashion modeling to bounty hunting. There's even a reality show about the making of a reality show!

With all these different takes on what real life looks like, you might start to wonder where you fit in. What's your reality? And more importantly, what is "God's reality" for your life?

In the pages that follow, you'll get the opportunity to discover some of life's great truths as revealed through your favorite reality shows. You'll also find God's take, as revealed in His Word, on the real-life issues you're dealing with now. From topics such as friendship, dating, and getting along with your parents to setting goals for the future and choosing a career—you'll find the wisdom of the Bible laid out in practical, easy-to-remember lists.

So lay that remote aside for a while and get ready to experience an exciting *Reality Check*.

SIMON SAYS

What Simon says has become the barometer for success for many contestants on the reality show that aims to find the next vocal music superstar. Through the course of a season, viewers will witness numerous changes in attire, musical style, and even personality among those competing for the coveted title, all based on popular opinion and the opinions of the handful of judges overseeing the contest.

Yet those who seem to do best in the competition are the people who come onto the show knowing who they are and what musical style suits them. The changes seen in them are only minor. They take hold of some of the constructive criticism and benefit from it, but then they take everything else for exactly what it is—personal opinion. They don't allow the opinions of others to measure their self-worth. They've found their voice and are comfortable with who they are.

Have you found your voice, or are you looking to others to show you how you should act, what you should wear, or what you should believe or think? It's tempting sometimes to try to

Have you found your voice, or are you looking to others to show you how you should act, what you should wear, or what you should believe or think?

act like someone we're not in order to gain the approval of others. In Shakespeare's *Hamlet*, Polonius gives young Laertes this wise advice: "This above all: to thine own self be true, and it must follow, as the night the day, thou canst not then be false to any man." In today's English, this could be restated, "Don't be a poser." Although this may be an over-simplification, what Shakespeare is saying through his character is to just be yourself, and you won't have to worry about what other people think of you.

You are a unique expression of God's creativity. He planted in you a combination of likes, dislikes, interests, and abilities that is yours alone. God is proud of who He made you, and He wants you to love who you are too. Be true to what you believe in, your values, and those things you really have a passion for. Even then, there will probably still be some people who, for whatever reason, don't like you. But that's their problem, not yours. And more importantly, you'll be able to know—and love—the person you spend most of your time with—yourself. So find your unique voice; then "sing" with confidence for the world to hear.

5 Roads to Popularity Without Losing Your Reputation

Everyone wants to be popular. Popularity isn't a bad thing. In fact, Jesus was very popular during much of His ministry. He never compromised His character or morals to gain acceptance. You can become popular by making both bad choices and good ones.

Here are 5 roads to popularity while maintaining your integrity.

1. Be a kind person. You will never be short on friends.

2. When you do something, do it with all your might. Excellence draws a crowd.

3. Promote others and their accomplishments, not your own. God will then be able to exalt you.

4. Dare to dream big and pray for the seemingly impossible. People are drawn to those filled with hope and faith.

5. Stand up for what is right. Our world today is desperately searching for real heroes.

5 Habits of Happy Teens

God wants you to be happy and enjoy life. That doesn't mean you will never experience trials or tough times. Here are 5 habits you can develop as a young person that will cause you to keep your joy through even the darkest hours.

1. Regularly reading and meditating (thinking and pondering) on God's Word. (Ps. 119:105.) This will energize your joy!

2. Steadily communing with God. "Communion" comes from the word "communicate." That's it! Talk to God, praise Him, and give Him your requests and cares.

3. Vision thinking. Find out what God has gifted you in. Take time to seek Him for your career and ambitions. Take one step at a time as you grow to get there.

4. Singing a good song aloud! God made us to sing. Not all of us sound that good, but it doesn't matter. Find songs and worship music that inspire you for good, and sing! (Ps. 95:1.)

5. Attending church weekly. Stay connected to good friends, strong mentors, and caring pastors who will help you stay on track.

6 Things You Must Believe About Yourself

You will eventually become a product of what you believe. All great athletes, presidents, pastors, and corporate CEOs arrived where they are because they believed they could before anyone else believed in them. Here are 6 things you must believe about yourself.

1. I have been given power over the devil. (1 John 4:4.)

2. I have been given power over every circumstance in my life. (Mark 11:23.)

3. I have a strong body that has been healed by the stripes taken on Jesus' back. (Matt. 8:17.)

4. I have the ability to control my mind and cast out evil thoughts. (2 Cor. 10:4-5.)

5. I am poised for success and will not accept any defeat as final. (1 Cor. 15:57.)

6. I hate sin but love all people and have favor everywhere I go. (Prov. 12:2.)

3 Ways to Discover Who You Are

Perhaps one of the greatest journeys that you'll ever take is the one that leads you to the discovery of who God created you to be. You have a unique personality and skill set that God has given you. Many young people fail to realize all that God has made them to be. Here are 3 things to remember in this exciting journey.

1. You will be incomplete without Christ. Maybe you recall the memorable scene in the Tom Cruise movie *Jerry McGuire* when Tom finds his wife, whom he had separated from earlier, and says to her, "You complete me." Just as God puts two people together in marriage, you are to be married to Christ. Without that ongoing relationship with Jesus, you will always come up short.

2. Study carefully what God has said about you. The Bible is full of Scriptures that describe the attributes and character that He has for you as a person. The Word of God is like a mirror. (James 1:23.) When you look at it and commit to do it, you take on the character of God.

3. Talk to family and friends about your unique personality. Many times other people see things in us that we fail to recognize. You may be a great organizer, counselor, leader, giver, creator, or helper, and people around you will see that more quickly than you most of the time.

3 Reasons Why Cool Doesn't Try—It Is

Truly cool people don't have to work at it—they just are. Let's be honest: If you have to try to be cool, you probably won't have a lot of people looking up to you. Let's check out 3 reasons why cool doesn't have to try.

1. Being cool is an honor that only others can bestow upon you. Remember, the Bible's counterparts for the modern word *cool* are *favored* and *accepted.* Only God and people can show you favor and acceptance.

2. Truly cool people focus on others, not on themselves. Matthew 23:12 says that those who humble themselves will be exalted.

3. Most cool people don't even realize they are cool. They're too busy making a difference in their world.

A MODEL OF CONFIDENCE

A new reality show produced by a famous supermodel gives thirty-nine hopeful girls a chance at becoming the next great rage within the cover girl scene. At first blush, these girls seem to exude confidence—in the way they walk, their posture, their facial expressions. And well they should, one might think. After all, each one of them is absolutely gorgeous, with perfect hair, perfect skin, and the perfect figure. And they certainly know their craft. As the host spouts off names of famous supermodels, they nail the most well-known pose for each model.

Yet the picture begins to change as the girls go before the panel of judges who pick them to pieces with their well-trained eyes. Instead of perfection, the judges see ears that are too big or too small, a smile that's not just right, a walk that simply doesn't work for modeling, or a look that's not "in" at the moment. Under such scrutiny, the confidence of many of the participants, which seemed so strong at the beginning of the show, now begins to crumble, and their insecurities begin to surface. Viewers learn that many of the young ladies are on the show because they feel a desperate need to prove themselves capable of succeeding to a friend or relative. From girl after girl come words to this effect: "This is my one shot. If I don't make it here, I don't know . . ." Her voice trails off and tears begin to flow. Sadly, in their teens or early twenties, many of these young ladies believe that they are getting their last chance at success, their one shot to prove they are good enough.

On what is your confidence based? Do your looks give you confidence? What about a special talent you have or your ability to make good grades in school? Perhaps you don't believe you have anything to be confident about.

The Bible talks a lot about confidence, but never as the result of some great look or talent within a person. Jeremiah 17:7 says, "Blessed is the man who trusts in the LORD, whose confidence is in him." Similarly, in Psalm 71:5, David states, "For you have been my hope, O Sovereign Lord, my confidence since my youth." If you've accepted God's gift of salvation and forgiveness, when He looks at you, He sees someone beautiful, righteous, blameless, and bursting with potential. Isaiah 32:17 promises, "The fruit of righteousness will be peace; the effect of righteousness will be quietness and confidence forever." If you'll place your confidence in God and in the way He sees you, you'll never have reason to hang your head.

5 Signs of a Confident Person

Use this as a check to see if you are confident in who you are in Christ.

1. You aren't afraid to meet new people.

2. You like to try new things and see new places.

3. You aren't afraid to take calculated risks in order to achieve something you want.

4. You don't get discouraged and depressed when you fail. Instead, you pick yourself back up.

5. It doesn't bother you much when people criticize you.

If all of the statements above describe you, you are very confident. If 4 of the statements are true about you, your confidence is solid and improving. Three true statements mean you could use some improvement. It's not looking good if only 2 statements are true; you are limiting yourself from great experiences. If you found only 1 statement to be true, reread this book every day until all the statements are true. Remember, in Christ you are a new creation. (2 Cor. 5:17.)

4 Differences Between Confidence and Arrogance

From a distance, arrogance can easily be mistaken for confidence. Here are 4 marks that make even the most confident person want to keep their distance from arrogance.

1. Confidence is based on a belief that whether I perform well or badly, I will be able to do whatever is next. Arrogance is based on appearance and performance and quickly dissolves in difficult circumstances.

2. Arrogance knows everything and refuses to be coached, even by the most knowledgeable person on even the smallest detail. Confidence is focused on continuing to improve and learning how to do better what you already do well.

3. Confidence means believing in yourself as you make the team better or strive to reach your goals. Arrogance is focused on yourself as you use the team or personal achievements to make yourself look better.

4. Arrogance treats the failures of others as catastrophic mistakes that you would never make. Confidence is using your talents and knowledge to make others better, not to make them feel smaller.

Reality Check

4 Ways to Discover What You Can Do

Proverbs 18:16 NASB promises, "A man's gift makes room for him and brings him before great men." Believe it or not, God has put special gifts of ability into your life. Here are 4 ways you can find out what they are.

1. Seek God in prayer, asking Him to reveal your abilities. Jeremiah 33:3 tells us when we call upon Him, He'll show us things to come.

2. Ask people close to you. Solicit the evaluation of friends, parents, teachers, coaches, and others you trust to give their observations on your gifting.

3. Go after things you have in your heart. Never be afraid to step out and attempt something you've never done.

4. Faithfully do the little things you are asked to do, the things you don't like as much. God promises to give you bigger things to do when you do the small stuff well. (Matt. 25:23.)

4 Reasons You Should Be Cool

God wants you to be cool, accepted, and favored. The Scripture says, "Let not mercy and truth forsake you; bind them around your neck, write them on the tablet of your heart, and so find favor and high esteem in the sight of God and man" (Prov. 3:3-4 NKJV). You can enjoy favor, acceptance, and popularity with both God and people. Here are 4 reasons why you should be cool.

1. Cool, accepted people have the ability to influence others for good. That includes a witness of your Christian faith.

2. Cool, favored people have confidence to do things others believe to be impossible or improbable.

3. Accepted people find it easy and natural to show others God's love and acceptance.

4. Cool people stand up for truth and don't need everyone to agree with them or even like them.

6 Ways Any Person Can Become Cool

Let's get right to the point: You want to be accepted and popular with people. Who doesn't? Now, you know you can't try to gain popularity and "coolness" the way the world tries to manufacture it. So how does a person become "Christ-like cool"?

1. You become cool when you stand up for what is right and don't care who stands with you.

2. You become cool when you reach out to the poor, the hurting, the lost—those who are "uncool."

3. You become cool when you take time for those whom many overlook—children. God loves kids, and so should we.

4. You become cool when you freely admit your shortcomings, pick up where you've failed, and move forward with godly confidence.

5. You become cool when you put God first in your words, your actions, and your plans.

6. You become cool when you couldn't care less about being cool.

3 Musts for Building Real Confidence

If you need more confidence in your life, here is a simple game plan that will help you grow.

1. Find your identity in Christ Jesus. If we look to ourselves for confidence, we have many reasons to be insecure and disappointed. But in Christ, we are amazing. Look up these Scriptures: 2 Corinthians 5:17; Philippians 4:13; Colossians 1:22; Jude 24; Romans 8:15.

2. Surround yourself with people who believe in you. Small people criticize big dreams. Don't allow your faith and self-esteem to be robbed by critical and negative people.

3. Take small steps to build big victories. We all have things in our lives we are secretly afraid of. Maybe it's heights, meeting new people, trying new foods, or sharing our faith. Don't take a leap of faith; take little steps toward overcoming your fears. The Bible says, "The steps of a good man are ordered by the Lord" (Ps. 37:23 KJV).

Build these 3 steps to confidence into your daily routine, and watch your confidence soar.

6 Enemies That Will Try to Steal Your Confidence

In battle, one of the best advantages you can have is to understand your enemy. The more you know your enemy, the better you can avoid his traps and attacks. Here are 6 enemies that will try to steal your confidence.

1. Negative people who criticize you. You get to choose who your friends are. If your friends pull you down, get new friends.

2. Unconfessed sin. This will rob your confidence before God. Don't be like Adam and Eve who hid from God. Go to Him, confess it, and be forgiven. (1 John 1:9.)

3. Listening to your feelings rather than God's Word. Feelings will betray you because they are subject to your circumstances. Fix your eyes on God's unchanging Word.

4. Looking at your past to determine your future. You may have a past littered with failure, but that doesn't mean you can't succeed. A righteous person falls 7 times but keeps getting back up. (Prov. 24:16.)

5. Looking at the problem rather than God's promise for the solution. God's Word has a promise for any problem you face.

6. Comparing yourself to other people. You are a great you but a lousy anyone else. Be you. You are great. (Jer. 1:5, 29:11; Ps. 138:8, 139.)

Don't let the enemy steal your confidence. You have every
reason to be secure. You're on God's team, and we win.

Reality Check

7 Scriptures That Prove God Is Confident in You

Here are 7 encouraging Scriptures to look up and commit to memory.

1. Psalm 138:8: God will fulfill His purpose for your life.

2. John 3:16: God believed in you enough to allow His Son, Jesus, to die for you.

3. Mark 16:15: After Jesus rose from the dead, He gave His ministry to His disciples and us to finish.

4. Jude 24: He said He will keep you from falling and present you in His presence with great joy.

5. Acts 1:8: He gave us His power and Holy Spirit to witness.

6. John 15:16: He handpicked you. You're His first-round draft pick.

7. Ephesians 2:5: Even while we were lost, He made us alive with Him.

If God is confident in you, that should be enough for you. He is the Creator of the universe, and He is on your side. You can't lose.

CLEAN YOUR ROOM!

If someone went into your room while you were away and started snooping through drawers and closets, what would they find out about you? A popular TV show does just that, only with a video camera, airing participants' "dirty laundry" to viewers nationwide. On each episode, a girl will rummage through the rooms of three guys, or a guy will go through the rooms of three girls. This person will then determine, based solely on the contents of the rooms, which person he or she would like to go out on a date with. It's amazing how much can be learned about someone by looking at his or her room. Posters, decorating style, organization (or lack of it), memorabilia, and clothing reveal much about a person's likes and dislikes, interests, passions, style, personality, and priorities.

Just as the things in your room speak volumes about you, the daily choices you make reflect what's in your heart. If someone followed you around for a day or a week observing your choices, would he or she see the same person you think you see when you look in the mirror?

The way you choose to spend your time reveals what's most important to you. Are the majority of your hours spent building your relationship with God and with other people and in preparing for a bright future, or do you find yourself putting those things off to play video games or watch TV for hours?

The people you choose to hang out with indicate what kind of person you strive to be. Do your friends embrace the same values you do, or do they tend to sway you toward doing things you know aren't right?

Your music, television, and movie choices are indicators of the contents of your thought life. Are you feeding your mind healthy images and lyrics on which to dwell?

Finally, the choices you make when you're in a clutch and are faced with an ethical dilemma speak volumes about your character. Are your actions any different when you think no one is watching?

Do your choices reflect the person you've determined in your heart to be? If not, maybe it's time to do some cleaning.

5 Decisions Young People Make That Sabotage Their Future

Who you are now and who you will be are determined by the decisions you make. One out of every one person will make decisions. When you have to make a decision and don't, that is in itself a decision. So the question is, what kind of decision-maker are you going to be? To help keep you from sabotaging your future, here are 5 decisions not to make.

1. Disobey your parents. God has placed your parents in your life to help guide you.

2. Make quick decisions. Before making a decision, take time to think it over.

3. Develop wrong relationships. The people you spend time with probably have the most influence on the decisions you make.

4. Wait for your big break. You must get off the couch and pursue your God-given destiny.

5. Give up. Both winners and losers face challenges, but winners don't quit.

3 Reasons Your Musical Choices Are Important

How many times have I heard teenagers tell me, when referring to blatantly immoral messages in their music, "Well, Pastor Blaine, I don't listen to the words, so they don't affect me." I understand what they are trying to say, and I do believe you can make good choices in spite of listening to bad music. But there are 3 reasons good choices are critical for each of us.

1. Messages, both good and evil, will have some effect on us. Why? Because the Bible teaches that there is power in words. Proverbs 23:7 teaches that as a man thinks in his heart, so is he. We are a product of our thoughts, and our thoughts are influenced by what we listen to in music or anything else.

2. Your witness and testimony for Christ are on the line each day. If you are listening to music that is exalting fornication, murder, rebellion, etc., what does that say about your devotion to Christ to others around you?

3. God's highest purpose for music is to facilitate worship and praise to Him in our lives. That's why an important part of the menu of music on your i Pod or in your CD case should be music that glorifies God and inspires you to serve Him.

4 Danger Zones in Modern Entertainment

I enjoy good entertainment just as much as the next guy, but I believe that we all must guard the gates of our minds and hearts. Second Timothy 3:1-6 says we are to have nothing to do with wicked and ungodly people. This biblical principle also applies to our entertainment.

Here are 4 danger zones that we must steer clear of in modern entertainment.

1. Sexual immorality. The Word of God says that there should not even be a hint of sexual immorality in our lives. (Eph. 5:3.) Have the courage not to compromise even when everyone else will.

2. Disrespect for authority. Honoring and obeying our parents will bring us blessings. (Ex. 20:12.) Paul wrote that our police, military, and government leaders are ministers of God. (Rom. 13:6.)

3. Mocking God. Did you know that when you fail to react to others who are degrading God and godly principles, you come into agreement with those acts? Jesus said that if you're ashamed of Him and the Word, He will be ashamed of you. (Luke 9:26.)

4. Rage. Don't believe that uncontrolled anger will bring a solution to your problem. It won't. It will add to your already existing problems. Proverbs 14:16 says, "A fool is hotheaded and reckless." Don't be a fool.

5 Ways to Have a Great Time Without Compromising

"Christians don't have any fun." That's the worst lie that's ever been pushed on young people in today's world! I've been a Christian since I was 16 years old, and I've had the time of my life the whole way. Let me give you 5 ways to get a life on the fast track.

1. Reach out and make some great friends with similar interests. Good friends can be a blast to hang out with. Laughing, talking, going places, learning how to live life together—it's awesome!

2. Find a hobby or activity you love. It may be a sport, collecting something, hunting, writing, acting, dancing—whatever. Just do something that you can look forward to.

3. Learn how to throw a great party without drugs, alcohol, and sex. A lot of Christian parties are boring because nothing is planned. It might be a great new game, karaoke, cooking everyone's favorite dish—just be creative!

4. Get into trouble that doesn't hurt anyone. It might be a great practical joke you and your friends play on somebody. Don't get me started. I love doing stuff like this!

5. Make a list of things you've never done or tried and want to do. Big stuff. Cool stuff. Now start making plans to check off everything on your list.

Reality Check

5 Scriptures to Guide Your Daily Entertainment Choices

In evaluating things we watch, listen to, or do, it is important to allow God to help you with decisions by comparing your choices to God's instruction. Believe it or not, the Bible has a lot to say about entertainment. Here are 5 awesome Scriptures to use in all your evaluations.

1. "Finally, brethren, whatever things are true, whatever things are noble, whatever things are just, whatever things are pure, whatever things are lovely, whatever things are of good report, if there is any virtue and if there is anything praiseworthy—meditate on these things" (Phil. 4:8 NKJV). What kind of thoughts is this producing in your life?

2. "And do not be conformed to this world, but be transformed by the renewing of your mind, that you may prove what is that good and acceptable and perfect will of God" (Rom. 12:2 NKJV). Is this causing you to conform to a worldly attitude or behavior?

3. "According to the eternal purpose which He accomplished in Christ Jesus our Lord" (Eph. 3:11 NKJV). Does it fall in line with God's purpose for your life?

4. "It is better to hear the rebuke of the wise than for a man to hear the song of fools" (Eccl. 7:5 NKJV). The Bible says a fool says, "There is no God." Is your entertainment denying the existence or goodness of God?

5. "And the tongue is a fire, a world of iniquity. The tongue is so set among our members that it defiles the whole body, and sets on fire the course of nature; and it is set on fire by hell" (James 3:6 NKJV). The tongue has power to destroy with the words it speaks. What kind of words are you allowing into your spirit?

FREE AT LAST!

On a reality show that's quickly gaining popularity, home-owners invite the show's designer into their home and give him permission to do whatever he desires as he and the show's team transform the home with a total makeover. This designer's style is anything but traditional. From an under-the-sea themed house—complete with a 250-gallon aquarium and a retractable periscope—to a mad-scientist house—featuring an electric chair and examination table—he takes creative freedom to a new level.

As you pass from childhood to your teen years and then into adulthood, you're probably gaining more and more freedom. What will you choose to do with that freedom?

Some people are afraid to become Christians while they are young because they believe that doing so will stifle their newfound freedom; when, in fact, just the opposite is true. The apostle Paul proclaimed, "It is for freedom that Christ has set us free" (Gal. 5:1). This and other bold statements Paul made during his ministry, such as, "You, my brothers, were called to be free" (Gal. 5:13) and "Everything is permissible" (1 Cor. 10:23), had religious leaders of the day in an outrage, wondering why Paul would encourage his followers to engage in a sinful lifestyle. Paul's message of freedom was in such sharp contrast to the legalistic, follow-every-letter-of-the-law-or-be-condemned-for-eternity religion of the day that it shocked people.

Of course, Paul was not telling people to go out and sin, as is evident in the warnings that follow each of his statements. Galatians 5:13 continues, "You, my brothers, were called to be free. But do not use your freedom to indulge the sinful nature; rather, serve one another in love." First Corinthians 10:23 goes on to say, "'Everything is permissible'—but not everything is beneficial. 'Everything is permissible'—but not everything is constructive." Paul wanted the early Christians to understand that they no longer had to try to earn their righteousness by following the letter of the law. Jesus had come and purchased their righteousness for them, so it no longer depended on them. They were accepted by God as soon as they believed in the power of the death and resurrection of Jesus.

The same is true for us today. We don't have to prove anything to God to be accepted by Him. Yet, while our salvation doesn't depend on following the commandments in the Bible, our happiness does. When we get caught up in doing things that are against what the Bible says—things like getting drunk, using drugs, gossip, lying—we actually lose our freedom. We become slaves to those things because we think we can't be ourselves without them. In contrast, when we follow what God says, not because we're afraid of punishment, but out of love for Him and because we're convinced that He wants what's best for us, we experience true freedom.

Paul calls God's Word "the perfect law that gives freedom" (James 1:25). Instead of thinking of the Bible as a rule book intended to do away with your freedom, use it as a field guide to get the most out of life and to make something beautiful out of the freedom you've been given.

2 Things Freedom Is Not

I was preaching at a crusade, and a young man walked up to me after the evening's events and said, "I don't listen to anyone. I do what I want, when I want, with whom I want to do it. I'm free!" I looked at him, trying to think of a way to shock him back into reality, and said, "Is that right? Well, I'm going to take that girl on your arm away from you tonight, and if you try to stop me, I'll dropkick you right in the face!" Of course, I wasn't serious…just setting up a point. He looked back and said, "Hey, you can't do that. That's wrong, man, to steal a guy's girl!" I smiled and said, "Hey, you're the one who said freedom is doing whatever you want, whenever you want, and I'm free too!" He got the point…which brings us to 2 things freedom is not.

1. Freedom is not a life without boundaries. Ask any prison inmate how much freedom they are enjoying after living outside the boundaries of the law.

2. Freedom is not getting away from your parents. Authority exists wherever you go, and you'd best learn to respect it. Your parents will likely be the kindest, most forgiving authority you'll ever have.

Reality Check

2 Mistakes Teenagers Make in a Desire for Freedom

I once heard a comedienne from the '70s and '80s make this proud statement: "The trouble with being in a rat race is that if you win the race, you're still a rat." The point is, you don't have to sneak, lie, and demand to get your way in life. Freedom attained by force and deception will be short-lived. Here are 2 critical mistakes young people make in their quest for living freely.

1. Comparing your freedoms to the freedoms of others. Have you ever said something like, "Well, all my friends get to do this. How come I'm the only one who can't?" The trap of comparisons will never end if you give in to it early in life. Learn to be content with the good things you already have.

2. Getting your freedom by deception. For example, telling your mom you're going one place and going somewhere else—the place she wouldn't let you go in the first place. Maybe you won't get caught, but you still have to live with yourself and your lies. And all your friends will know you can't be trusted—you'll deceive your own mother if necessary. The Bible says that the truth will set you free. (John 8:32.) Truthfulness brings trust; and trust secures freedom.

3 Freedoms You Are Entitled to Every Day

Men and women have given their lives so that you and I can enjoy the life we have today. The freedom we enjoy in America is stained with the blood of soldiers who died for the rights we often take for granted. God sent His Son, Jesus, to give us eternal freedoms that no one can take away from us. Here are 3 freedoms that you might fight to keep.

1. The freedom to worship God. I've had students whose parents have told them they couldn't go to church and be a Christian. I've told those students that they must obey their higher authority—God Almighty—and to respectfully explain to their parents that they have made a decision to live for Christ and cannot retreat.

2. The freedom to share your faith. More and more in America, ungodly groups of people are trying to limit the expression of faith in any public venue. It won't be long until they try to tell us what we can do in our own homes! In spite of their efforts, we have the God-given right to proclaim the goodness of God to all people wherever we go. (Mark 16:15.)

3. The freedom to learn. There are many countries around the world whose citizens are told what they are allowed to learn. Many have no libraries, no communication tools, no higher education. You have been given the right to discover all that you need to make your life all that it can be. Use it!

3 Sacrifices That Will Guarantee Freedom

You can get a lot of things for free in life. Those AOL CDs at the grocery store. Mints at a restaurant. Real estate booklets at the convenience store. But one thing I can promise you is not free are freedoms. There is work and sacrifice you must make to gain new freedom. This is true with your parents, with your work career, or with any other area of life. Here are 3 sacrifices you must be willing to make.

1. The sacrifice of honesty. Even when it hurts you, honesty must be a value you hold true to. When you develop a reputation for always being honest, even when it's to your detriment, people will trust you with freedoms not afforded to others.

2. The sacrifice of diligence. When your parents see you do your homework, yard work, chores, or part-time job well and without complaints, your freedoms will rise.

3. The sacrifice of servanthood. Stop demanding your rights, and start serving others' requests. When you develop a heart that is "others first," others will start to put "you first."

CAN YOU REALLY WIN BY LOSING?

Since when has being called a big loser been considered a symbol of honor? For some, it's been since a popular TV reality show set out to help people lose weight and achieve a healthier lifestyle. Over the course of a five-month period, fourteen contestants, divided into two teams, are pushed to the extreme to see how much weight they can lose. Each team has a professional trainer who leads them through a series of exercises for hours each day. They must complete challenges and are taught how to choose healthy foods and to resist junk food. At the end of each episode there is a weigh-in, and the team with the least percentage of weight loss has to vote off one of their team members. The last person standing is then granted the esteemed title of champion "loser" and receives a $250,000 prize.

Giving the prize to the loser may seem like a bit of a paradox. But, in fact, being a loser had a positive side long before this show came into existence. Jesus said, "Whoever loses his life for my sake will find it" (Matt. 10:39). This statement comes at the end of Jesus' instructions to His disciples when He sent them out on their own to minister for the first time. His words wouldn't be considered much of a motivational speech by today's standards. At one point He tells His disciples, "I am sending you out like sheep among wolves" (Matt. 10:16). Later, He goes on to say, "All men will hate you because of me" (Matt. 10:22). Still, the disciples went willingly because they had seen from Jesus' example the value of being a servant—of placing the needs of others before their own.

When some of the disciples later forgot this lesson and began to argue about who was the greatest among them, Jesus spoke these words to them: "Whoever wants to become great among you must be your servant, and whoever wants to be first must be your slave—just as the Son of Man did not come to be served, but to serve, and to give his life as a ransom for many" (Matt. 20:26-28).

By the world's standards, Jesus wouldn't be considered much of a success. He was born in a stable to a common carpenter, quit his job to travel around preaching to people—probably depending on the goodness of His followers for food and shelter, and died the death of the worst kind of criminal. Yet we know Him as the King of kings, Lord of lords, and Conqueror of death and sin. He lived a life of service and wants us to do the same.

So, go ahead; be a big loser. It's the losers who will gain the ultimate prize—eternal, abundant life.

5 Unselfish Acts in the Bible

Do you need a role model of unselfishness? The stories of the Bible have been placed there for our example. Let's take a look at 5 unselfish acts we can imitate.

1. Abraham and Isaac. (Gen. 22.) Abraham was willing to give his beloved son for the cause of God.

2. The crucifixion of Christ. (Matt. 27.) Jesus Christ, being without sin, died the death of a criminal so that we could live a life free from sin.

3. Joseph and his brothers. (Gen. 37-45.) Joseph did not strike back in vengeance towards his brothers, who sold him into slavery, when he had the opportunity to do so.

4. The poor widow. (Luke 21:1-4.) Although poor, this widow gave all she could give.

5. The Good Samaritan. (Luke 10:30-36.) This Samaritan acted unselfishly, regardless of what others might have thought.

4 Reasons People Become Selfish

Have you ever wondered how someone could be so selfish? To answer that question and to help you avoid that same pitfall, here is a list of 4 reasons why people become selfish.

1. They make the choice to be selfish. We must make a decision not to be selfish, even if we don't feel like it. I have found that as you act on your decision, the feelings will come.

2. They take for granted the joy of giving. Not only will an unselfish act bring joy to others, but the giver will receive joy as well.

3. They have unrenewed thinking. We're all born naturally selfish, but that doesn't mean we must stay that way. We need to put selfless thoughts in and selfish thoughts out.

4. They're unthankful. Unthankfulness will cause people to become selfish. People who are unthankful stop recognizing the goodness of others; therefore, they develop an unwillingness to give.

4 Qualities of a Great Teammate

Ordinary teams become successful when individuals understand what it means to be a teammate. Here are 4 qualities that will help your team by helping you become an extraordinary teammate.

1. Great teammates know their role. Anything that has more than one part needs definition in order to be put together properly. If you don't know your role on a team, then you will never know if you are playing the right part or doing what it takes to play your part well.

2. Great teammates take care of the responsibilities. Once you know your role, work hard on your responsibilities in that role. You will earn the respect of your team and coaches as you prove that you will be where you are supposed to be and doing what you are supposed to be doing. Your team needs to know that they can count on you to take care of your part while they are doing theirs.

3. Great teammates make others look good. If you focus only on your stats, your numbers, your percentages, or making yourself look good, you will quickly alienate your team and begin to lose their respect. Instead, look for ways to make your teammates look good at practice, at school, and during the game.

4. Help your team improve by helping your teammates improve. Working on your skills and ability may add to the effectiveness of your team, but working with your team to improve

collectively will multiply your ability to produce great results. No matter what your skill level is right now, by helping the lesser players or pushing the greater players, you can help your team in some way.

5 Ways to Lead Without Being a Captain

Leadership does not begin when you are given a title. It is a process that begins long before you are ever placed in a position or given official authority. These are 5 ways you can begin to lead now without being a captain.

1. Support your coaches and team captains. Anyone can be supportive when you win, but what are you doing and saying to support your team leaders during difficulty or when they aren't around? Your commitment to the team will show in what you do when something goes wrong or when a decision isn't popular.

2. Volunteer for extra duties/assignments. Be the first one to speak up when a special need is spotted or when your coach or captain needs an extra hand.

3. Keep a positive attitude. No matter how difficult a practice or how badly you are losing during a game, staying positive will help your teammates keep going. A positive attitude is contagious; unfortunately, so is a negative one.

4. Lead by example. Show up early, work hard, do things to the best of your ability, and be prepared when it's your turn to perform. Leading by example means doing what you would expect your coach or captain to do in the same circumstance.

5. Go the extra mile to create team unity. Think of ways to build relationships with the members of your team. Find time to get to know something about each person on your team. The better you know your team away from the game, the better you will know them when it comes time to play.

WHO LET THE "DOG" OUT?

An interesting concept in reality TV is a show that documents the daily life of a bounty hunter and his family. One peculiarity on the show is that each time the family gets ready to go out on a job, the father gathers them together to pray. It's not something one would expect from such a rough-looking guy. In fact, it's in stark contrast to the language he uses while chasing down his intended target. Yet, once he captures the person he's after, viewers get another surprise. All the way to the jailhouse, he counsels the people he captures with an obviously genuine concern for their well-being. He advises them in no uncertain terms to stop wasting their lives and tells them they're better than the way they're living.

So can God use a tattoo-covered bounty hunter to further the gospel? In the Bible, God used all kinds of people to do good. His disciple Matthew was a tax collector, one of a group hated for their dishonest dealings. David, the one he called a man after His own heart, had a man killed in order to steal his wife.

You see, when God forgives us, He doesn't expect us to become perfect overnight. In fact, He knows perfection is impossible for us, and, what's more, He designed it that way. First Corinthians 1:28-30 (NLT) says, "God chose things despised by the world, things counted as nothing at all, and used them to bring to nothing what the world considers important, so that no one can ever boast in the presence of God. God alone made it possible for you to be in Christ Jesus. . . . He is the one who made us acceptable to God. He made us pure and holy, and he gave himself to purchase our freedom." He's made it impossible for us to be good enough on our own so that we won't start boasting and stop relying on His love and forgiveness.

That's not to say that we can never stop doing bad things. As we place our trust in His love and accept His forgiveness, His Holy Spirit works in our hearts and shows us areas that need to be changed. Then He gives us all the strength we need to overcome those habits.

Realize the power of God's forgiveness in your life, and see how He can use you now, faults and all. Then pass that forgiveness on to those around you. Don't be too quick to judge people because of their hang-ups. When you choose to see the good in others, you just may find a blessing somewhere you never would have thought to look.

4 Steps to Finding Favor With God

Let's be honest. If you can get yourself in favor with the most powerful Person in the universe, you're going to do really well. The great thing is that God has told us clearly in His Word that we can fall into favor with Him. Here are 4 steps to getting there.

1. Diligently seek after Him. He promises to reward and bless anyone who wholeheartedly seeks Him. (Heb. 11:6.)

2. Search out the wisdom of God's Word. He promises that when we discover His wisdom we will obtain favor from Him. (Prov. 8:35.)

3. Develop a lifestyle of praising God without apology. The churches in the book of Acts were bold to praise God with their voices and found favor with all the people. (Acts 2:47.)

4. Walk into goodness and integrity towards others. God promises you favor but condemns the person who is wicked in one's actions. (Prov. 12:2.)

7 Things God Did in Loving Us

God did not love us in word only. There wasn't a thundering voice from heaven one day for all of humanity to hear: "I am God. I love you. Any questions?" No, He has proved His love to us in so many ways. Here are 7 ways we should never forget.

1. He sent His only Son to pay the penalty of sin for us all. (John 3:16.)

2. He promised us the power of the Holy Spirit to live this life for Him every day. (Acts 1:8.)

3. He gave us the Church so that we would not have to make it through life by ourselves. (1 Cor. 12:27.)

4. He gave us His Word to guide us, strengthen us, and inspire us each day. (Ps. 119:105.)

5. He gave us gifts and talents that will bless others and prosper us. (Prov. 18:16.)

6. He promised to never allow us to be tempted or tested beyond our abilities to resist and overcome. (1 Cor. 10:13.)

7. He gave us the gift of heaven. Even on our worst days on this earth, we have the promise of eternal life and an eternal city with no pain, no tears...only good! (Rev. 21:4.)

2 Reasons You May Not Feel Forgiven

When you accept God's forgiveness and confess Jesus as Lord, you are forgiven of all of your sins. (Rom. 10:9-10.) Although you receive a new spirit, your soul (which is made up of your mind, will, and emotions) remains the same. Paul tells us in Romans 12:2 that we must actively renew our minds by spending time in God's Word. Because this is something that we must do ourselves, it does not happen overnight. It takes time for your soul to match up with your spirit. Here are 2 reasons you may not feel forgiven.

1. Your thoughts. Once you have confessed your sins, God has promised that He has forgiven you. (1 John 1:9.) Your thoughts, however, will try to tell you otherwise. Because your mind must be continually renewed, you may still have doubts about your forgiveness. You may even think that perhaps God didn't hear your prayer. But no matter what your thoughts tell you, you must believe God's Word over what you think.

2. Your emotions. Emotions can be a wonderful thing. They can add excitement as you anticipate an upcoming event and make you happy when something good happens. But emotions can bring you down in negative circumstances and leave you feeling depressed if something bad happens. As you accept God's forgiveness, your emotions may not confirm that forgiveness. You may still fight feelings of guilt over things you've done in the past. However, the truth is you are forgiven no matter what your emotions tell you. As you trust God and continue to obey His Word, your emotions will begin to line up with the truth of God's Word.

3 Ways to Know That You Have Not Committed the Unpardonable Sin

Perhaps you have heard the term 'unpardonable sin' and thought to yourself, *I feel far away from God; how can He forgive me?* or, *How do I know that I haven't sinned too much to be forgiven?* Jesus refers to the sin that isn't forgivable in Matthew 12:31-32. As Jesus was teaching and casting out demons, the religious leaders accused Him of doing this by satanic means. They were so spiritually blind that they gave credit for the work of the Holy Spirit to Satan. It was then Jesus said, "Every sin and blasphemy will be forgiven men, but the blasphemy against the [Holy] Spirit will not be forgiven" (v. 31). So the unpardonable sin is not simply saying an unkind word about the Holy Spirit; it is rejecting God altogether and being so hard-hearted that you don't know the difference between evil and good. The unpardonable sin is not unforgivable because God doesn't want to forgive it, but because He cannot forgive someone who has rejected Him altogether. Here are 3 ways to know that you have not committed the unpardonable sin.

1. You have a desire to serve God. If you want to be obedient to God's Word and serve Him, then God's forgiveness is still available to you. It is those who have hardened their hearts and do not want to receive from God who cannot enjoy His mercy.

2. You repent and recognize your need for forgiveness. When you acknowledge your sin and ask God for forgiveness, you

become humble and automatically take yourself out of the company of those who are too hard-hearted to turn from sin.

3. You recognize the difference between good and evil. The religious leaders in Matthew 12 were so blinded that when Jesus was doing good, they accused Him of working through the power of Satan. When you go to God and say, "God, I recognize that You are holy and that in order to have a relationship with You, my sins have to be forgiven," you are acknowledging that God is good. If you desire for the Holy Spirit to work in your life, you can be at peace knowing that you haven't committed the unpardonable sin.

7 Bible Guarantees
for Forgiveness

The foundational element of the Bible is God's plan of redemption for mankind. Throughout the pages of God's Word, you can find His desire for you to be saved. God loved you so much that He did everything to provide forgiveness for you, except make you receive it. That one small part is yours to play. God's forgiveness is available for you today. Here are 7 promises from the Bible that guarantee your forgiveness.

1. God's Word guarantees that forgiveness is available to everyone regardless of background. (Rom. 10:13 KJV.) Acts 10:34 KJV says, "Of a truth I perceive that God is no respecter of persons." No matter who you are or where you are from, God's forgiveness is available to you.

2. God's Word guarantees that if you repent, you will be forgiven. First John 1:9 KJV says, "If we confess our sins, he is faithful and just to forgive us our sins, and to cleanse us from all unrighteousness." Forgiveness is obtained by a choice you make to receive God's gift. Although forgiveness is free, it is possible only if you humble yourself, admit you were wrong, and acknowledge your need for God.

3. God's Word guarantees that you are forgiven when you choose to forsake your sin. Proverbs 28:13 NKJV says, "He who covers his sins will not prosper, but whoever confesses and forsakes them will have mercy." God's desire is that you forsake the things that cause you to stumble and grow in a relationship with Him each day.

4. God's Word guarantees that Jesus paid the price for your forgiveness so that you don't have to. Second Corinthians 5:21 NKJV says, "For He made Him who knew no sin to be sin for us, that we might become the righteousness of God in Him." By taking our punishment for us, Jesus made a way for us to be forgiven. There is no debt left to pay; it's been paid in full.

5. God's Word guarantees that we're forgiven by faith, not by works. Ephesians 2:8-9 NKJV says, "For by grace you have been saved through faith, and that not of yourselves; it is the gift of God, not of works, lest anyone should boast." It's not by your own strength or anything that you've done that you are forgiven. There is nothing you can do to earn your way into heaven. You can't be good enough, work hard enough, or buy your way into heaven. It is simply by the work of Jesus dying on the cross and rising again that you have been forgiven.

6. God's Word guarantees that when you are forgiven, God no longer remembers your sin. Hebrews 10:17 NKJV says, "...'Their sins and their lawless deeds I will remember no more.'" God's forgiveness is a complete work. The slate is wiped clean. The sin is remembered no more.

7. The Bible guarantees that God desires to forgive you because of His love for you. Romans 8:32 NKJV says, "He who did not spare His own Son, but delivered Him up for us all, how shall He not with Him also freely give us all things?" God's love for you is so great that He gave His own Son to pay the price for your forgiveness. No one forced God to provide a way of forgiveness. He did it because He loves you.

THE ULTIMATE MAKEOVER

On one popular reality show, participants go to extreme meas-
ures to change their outward appearance. After going through
an extensive series of surgeries—rhinoplasty, liposuction, hair
implants, neck sculpting, tummy tucks, chemical peels—
participants are sent to the show's mansion to recover. When
the painful two-month recovery period is complete and the new
looks are revealed, many are thrilled to have the look they'd
always dreamed of. Whether the happiness gained through
this painstaking process has long-term results is widely
debated. Some participants claim to have a new outlook on life
because of the confidence they gained through the changes to
their physical appearance. Others are happy at first but soon
find other areas of their physical appearance they don't like
and never seem to be completely satisfied.

Do you feel the need for a major transformation in your life?
If so, there's no need to join the masses who wait in line for
days to be considered as a candidate for this reality show or
to subject your body to such a grueling process. Jesus was in

the business of transforming lives long before plastic surgery was an option, and His methods have never been outdone. He works from the inside out—softening your heart so you'll be more approachable to others, revealing to you the perfection and beauty He sees when He looks at you, showing you your right to confidence as a child of the living God.

When you place your heart in God's hands and allow Him to sculpt you into a new person, He doesn't subject you to the painful process of exposing faults and then cutting into them. Instead, He gently leads you toward those things He knows will be best for you. He may change your focus, but that new focus will be more in line with the activities and interests you enjoy. He may even reveal to you abilities you never realized you had. You'll notice your desires being focused more toward relationships and helping others—those things that will have eternal value.

So before you entrust your life to the hands of a plastic surgeon, consider placing that trust instead in the hands of the Great Physician, your Creator, who wants only the best for you, and who can make you beautiful and complete not just externally but on the inside as well.

3 Things God's Love Does to People

We cannot really love others the way God intended unless we have embraced His love for us. You cannot give something away that you do not have in the first place. God wants you to be filled to overflowing with His love so that you can pour out His goodness to others. Here are 3 things God's love will do for you and for those you have the opportunity to influence.

1. God's love covers all sin. Proverbs says that love covers a multitude of sin. There is no sin too great that, if you sincerely repent and are sorry, God will not remove as if it never existed. People need to know that the blood Jesus shed on the cross has the power to cleanse even the worst of sinners.

2. God's love covers all people. Republicans. Democrats. Independents. Americans. Canadians. Chinese. Rich. Poor. Famous. Obscure. Red. Yellow. Black. White. As the song goes, we are all precious in His sight. In God's eyes, we are all one class of people. His creation. He loves us all without discrimination.

3. God's love covers all the time. Going to church is awesome. I believe it ought to be a weekly habit in our lives. But God's love is available to us and to others 7 days a week. Don't wait for Sunday for God to minister to you. Don't wait for Sunday to reach out to someone around you. His love is always in the now!

3 Ways to Lift Jesus Up in Your World

How do I lift Jesus up in my world? Wear a big Christian T-shirt that says, "You're going to hell—ask me how!" Right? Well, maybe not. Not to say that the entire Christian T-shirt industry needs to shut down, but maybe just some of it. The world is looking for more of a witness than a cute little message printed on 100 percent cotton. There are real ways that you can lift up Jesus in a real world. Here are a few.

1. Go the extra mile in all your work. Whether it's a job at McDonald's, early-morning cheerleading or football practice, a biology class, or chores for your parents, give all you have and a little extra in all you do. This practice, when done consistently, will eventually provoke questions by curious observers, giving you the chance to share your reasons and faith.

2. Put a watch on your words. Guard your tongue, seeking to edify, encourage, and promote wholesome conversation. Refuse to gossip and betray the trust people have in your friendship. You will stand out from the crowd and will soon be given the chance to explain why.

3. Break out of your comfort zone. Help a stranger in need. Introduce yourself to a neighbor. Take a coworker out for lunch. Make a new friend. Each time you step into the life of someone else, incredible opportunities to share Christ are likely to follow.

5 Keys to Keep Christ First

If we seek to save our lives, we will lose them; but if we lose our lives for Christ's sake, we will find them. (Luke 17:33.) This is somewhat of a paradox, but it is absolutely the truth. It's only when we truly allow Jesus to take all the controls of our lives that things will really take off in the right direction.

Here are 5 keys to keeping Christ first.

1. Fill your mind with good, life-giving information. The Bible, good books, and edifying music are just some of the things that can help keep your focus on the Lord.

2. Pray regularly. Make God your best friend, not the heavenly rescue team that you call on only when you're in trouble.

3. Keep good Christian friends. Proverbs 13:20 NKJV says that the companion of fools will be destroyed. Avoid the fools.

4. Stay committed to your local church. Christians are unable to survive alone. We are called to be connected to the Body of Christ in a local church. Go every week, and get involved.

5. Get rid of sin and weights. Hebrews 12:1 teaches us that if we want to finish the race God has called us to run, we must lay aside our sin and the weights that may hold us back. You know if there's something holding you back. Leave it behind.

7 Personal Beliefs That Will Alter Your Future

Without a doubt, the most important thing you can establish in your life right now is what you believe. Your core convictions will separate you from the pack.

Here are 7 beliefs from the Bible that, if acted on, will alter your future for good.

1. I believe I am God's child and He is my Father. (1 John 3:1.)

2. I believe the Holy Spirit leads me in all my decisions. (Rom. 8:14.)

3. I believe I am more than a conqueror in every challenge life brings. (Rom. 8:37.)

4. I believe God is the Author of my promotion in every area of life. (Ps. 75:6-7.)

5. I believe that when I pray, God hears me and answers me. (Mark 11:24.)

6. I believe that as I meditate on God's Word, He makes my way prosperous. (Josh. 1:8.)

7. I believe that nothing is impossible because I believe. (Mark 9:23.)

3 Daily Habits to Grow in Your Relationship With God

Habits make or break us. In fact, our lives are by-products of the daily habits we form. Research has said it takes 21 days to form a habit. Take the next 3 weeks to build these 3 habits in your life, and watch your walk with God grow.

1. At breakfast each morning, read one chapter of Proverbs. By the time you're done eating, you will have easily read a chapter.

2. Find one Scripture in the chapter you read that really stands out to you. Write it down on a piece of paper or a 3 x 5 index card and carry it with you wherever you go.

3. Whenever you hit slow times in your day, such as being stuck in traffic on the school bus, pull out the card and meditate on your Scripture.

Commit these 3 simple habits to your life, and you will grow rapidly.

AN AMAZING JOURNEY

You've probably tuned in to watch as teams of all different walks of life embark on a race around the globe striving to win a million-dollar prize. They are led by clues to their next destination all along the way and don't know until they get to the next checkpoint where, or even if, they will be sleeping that night. They could be camping out with only a sleeping bag in the desert, or they might spend the night on a plane headed for a different country. Along the way, they are required to overcome many challenges and aren't allowed to proceed until they've conquered the challenge. They never know what's coming next but must get through every challenge to stay in the competition.

What would happen if a team decided they would take a different route from where the clues were leading them— maybe avoid a few of the challenges and get to the next destination more quickly? Their role in the competition would undoubtedly be short-lived, because the show doesn't work that way. It's not so much about the destination as it is about everything the contestants encounter along the way.

Our lives are much like this race. God has a plan laid out for us, but He doesn't let us in on it all at once. Instead, He gives us clues along the way. We encounter challenges, and these challenges often help prepare us for events coming later on down the road.

It's tempting to think that life would be so much easier if God would just let us in on His whole plan for us now. Have you ever told yourself, "If I just knew God's will, I would do it"? But if we knew exactly where God was leading us and everything that would happen along the way, would we brave the challenges ahead, or would we try to find our own route to the destination God has for us?

One interesting phenomena about this show is that, in the end, no one goes home empty-handed. Only one team wins the million dollars, but often the greatest rewards are a result of having taken the journey—mended relationships, self-revelation, confidence, changed lives. As you seek after God's purpose for your life, be content to learn as you go, and allow yourself to enjoy the journey.

4 Ways God Gives You Direction

Do you need direction? Good, because God wants to give it to you. The direction of God is not hard to come by. Here are 4 ways He will give it to you.

1. The Word (Bible): the most practical way that God gives direction. All other ways must line up with this way.

2. Peace: how God will lead you. His peace will be deep down inside letting you know you're headed in the right direction.

3. People: pastors, teachers, parents, and friends. God will speak through these people whom He has strategically placed in your life.

4. Desires: what you want to do. Do you like making art, building, or helping others? God has placed desires in your heart to help give you direction.

7 Absolutes of God's Will for Your Life

Have you ever heard someone say, "God moves in mysterious ways"? I sure am glad that statement isn't true. The will of God doesn't have to be mysterious. Here are 7 things you can absolutely count on.

1. God's will is salvation. Our heavenly Father desires that all of humankind have eternal life with Him. That includes you.

2. God's will is dominion. Dominion simply means control. God wants you to apply His Word and take control of your body, thought life, attitude, and future.

3. God's will is discipleship. We are to grow in our walk with Christ. As we mature, we are to help others do the same.

4. God's will is unity. Your words and actions must be united with God's Word.

5. God's will is stewardship. We are to take proper care of our time, money, abilities, and all God has entrusted us with.

6. God's will is relationships. Through the power of relationships, you will be able to accomplish things that would be impossible if you were alone.

7. God's will is progressive. God has a plan for your life that will be completed one step at a time, not in leaps or bounds.

7 Scriptures to Guide Your Future

Can you imagine going into an uncharted forest without any map or compass? You might be lost for years. Many young people are living lost lives because they have thrown down the compass of the Word of God. Memorize these Scriptures. Pray them over your future and let them guide you.

1. Jeremiah 29:11 NKJV: "For I know the thoughts that I think toward you, says the Lord, thoughts of peace and not of evil, to give you a future and a hope."

2. Jeremiah 33:3 NKJV: "'Call to Me, and I will answer you, and show you great and mighty things, which you do not know.'"

3. Joshua 1:8 NKJV: "This Book of the Law shall not depart from your mouth, but you shall meditate in it day and night, that you may observe to do according to all that is written in it. For then you will make your way prosperous, and then you will have good success."

4. Proverbs 18:16 NKJV: "A man's gift makes room for him, and brings him before great men."

5. Ephesians 3:20-21 NKJV: "Now to Him who is able to do exceedingly abundantly above all that we ask or think, according to the power that works in us, to Him be glory."

6. 2 Timothy 1:9 NKJV: "[God] has saved us and called us with a holy calling, not according to our works, but according to His own purpose and grace which was given to us in Christ Jesus before time began."

7. Ephesians 5:15 NKJV: "See then that you walk circumspectly, not as fools but as wise."

5 Sources of Reliable Counsel

It is important to carefully choose who and what you allow to influence your choices. Some people will have good intentions but lead you astray with their advice. God has placed specific people in your life to speak into your decision-making. There are sources that you should always go to when you are in need of counsel. Here are 5 great sources of reliable counsel.

1. The Bible. Psalm 32:8 says, "I will instruct you and teach you in the way you should go; I will counsel you and watch over you." The Bible is full of answers to life's most difficult problems. If you are searching for an answer, the Bible is the first place you should look. You should always judge any other advice by what the Bible has to say.

2. Parents. God chose your parents to raise you and teach you as you grow and mature. Godly parents are a blessing, but even if your parents aren't Christians, they can still be a great source of answers to practical questions.

3. Mentor. If you don't have a solid parental figure in your life, maybe there is someone you look up to, such as a teacher or coach. Mentors can often provide an objective viewpoint and help you see the whole picture.

4. Pastor. God has placed leaders in the church to act as shepherds over believers. As shepherds, it is their job to protect, nurture, and lead you as a Christian. They can be a great source of biblical wisdom and godly counsel.

5. Holy Spirit. Jesus gave you the Holy Spirit as your Comforter. He is always with you and will never leave you. John 14:26 NKJV says, "He will teach you all things, and bring to your remembrance all things that I said to you."

Reality Check

4 Things to Look for in a Mentor

A mentor is critical in the life of every successful person. Joshua had Moses. Elisha had Elijah. The disciples had Jesus. Oftentimes, mentors won't seek you out—you'll have to find them. Here are 4 clues in finding the right one for you.

1. A good track record. Look for someone who has a good history of success in the thing you want to do.

2. Mutual benefit. Every great relationship will be good for both people. It is never one-sided. What can you do to help this potential mentor, bringing benefit to them?

3. Unforced relationship. Allow the mentoring relationship to develop naturally. Don't try to force someone into this. Just find a way to be around them by serving, helping, and contributing any way you can.

4. Ask the right questions at the right time. Don't overwhelm this person to the point that they want to avoid you. Be sensitive to the right opportunities to learn. Most of the time, you'll learn more by observing them.

4 Steps to Knowing God's Leading

God has promised that He will lead and guide those who diligently follow Him. (Prov. 3:5-6.) There are times when you
face a decision and you're not sure which way to go. When
there doesn't seem to be a definite right answer, here are 4
questions to ask yourself.

1. "Do I have peace about it?" If you are born again, God has
   promised that the Holy Spirit will lead and guide you into all
   truth. (John 16:13.) James 3:17 NKJV says, "But the wisdom that
   is from above is first pure, then peaceable...." If it is not a question of right and wrong, the next step is to follow peace.

2. "Does it line up with God's Word?" God's Word is constant. (Ps.
   119:89.) It is settled. So you will never get a leading that
   contradicts what God has said in His Word. The Bible is full of
   wisdom that will help you make good choices.

3. "Is it a step or a leap?" Psalm 37:23 NKJV says, "The steps of a
   good man are ordered by the Lord." God leads one step at a
   time. He will never ask you to do more than you are able. If it
   feels like a leap, it probably is. Take a step back and reevaluate
   the situation.

4. "Is it mutually beneficial?" God's kingdom operates on a
   system of exchange. Sowing and reaping, springtime and
   harvest, and labor and pay are all examples of exchange. God
   will not lead you to do something that requires you to sacrifice everything without compensation. Long-term, overseas
   missionaries, for example, have to make sacrifices in order to
   spread the gospel. But God will not ask you to be a full-time

missionary without also giving you ways and means to take care of your family in exchange for being obedient. God knows what you need and will be faithful to provide. (Matt. 6:33.) In Matthew 10:10 NKJV, Jesus said, "A worker is worthy of his food." When God directs you to do something, there will be something beneficial that you bring to the relationship and something good that you take away.

7 Bible Guarantees for Direction

A lack of direction causes many people to wander aimlessly through life. Without direction, it is impossible to know whether or not you are getting anywhere or accomplishing your goals. God has promised throughout His Word that He will guide and direct us. Here are 7 Bible guarantees for direction.

1. The Bible guarantees that if you trust in God, He will direct your path. Proverbs 3:5-6 NKJV says, "Trust in the Lord with all your heart, and lean not on your own understanding; in all your ways acknowledge Him, and He shall direct your paths." When you limit God's leading to your understanding, you rule out hidden potential. But by acknowledging God in all that you do, you open the door for Him to lead you even if you don't understand it all right away.

2. The Bible guarantees that God has a plan for your life. Jeremiah 29:11 NKJV says, "For I know the thoughts that I think toward you, says the Lord, thoughts of peace and not of evil, to give you a future and a hope." This guarantee can strengthen your faith, knowing that God has great things in store for you. God will never forget about you, and no matter where you are, God sees you and has a plan for your success.

3. The Bible guarantees that God will direct the steps of the righteous man. Psalm 37:23 NKJV says, "The steps of a good man are ordered by the Lord, and He delights in his way." Even though you can't see 50 years into your future, God has guaranteed that He will direct the steps that are in front of you.

4. The Bible guarantees that the Lord's purpose for you will prevail. Proverbs 19:21 NKJV says, "There are many plans in a man's heart, nevertheless the Lord's counsel—that will stand." No matter what you face or how many people let you down, God's direction and plan for your life will stand strong. Your path to God's best is not dependent on what other people do or what breaks you catch; it is dependent on your faithfulness to God, and God will never let you down.

5. The Bible guarantees that the plans of the diligent lead to plenty. Proverbs 21:5 NKJV says, "The plans of the diligent lead surely to plenty, but those of everyone who is hasty, surely to poverty." The Bible promises that if you are diligent and do your part to follow God's direction, the path will always lead to abundance.

6. The Bible guarantees that if you remain humble, God will guide you. Psalm 25:9 NKJV says, "The humble He guides in justice, and the humble He teaches His way." If you remain humble, you allow God to continually teach and instruct you throughout your life. But if you become proud and unteachable, you limit God's ability to guide you as you grow.

7. The Bible guarantees that His children will be led by His Spirit. Romans 8:14 NKJV says, "For as many as are led by the Spirit of God, these are sons of God." You become a son (or daughter) of God when you are born again. As a child of God, you have a supernatural ability to be led by the Spirit of God. You can stand on His Word, knowing that even in difficult situations, He will be there to lead and guide you.

4 Ways to Discover Your Life's Calling

Studies have proven again and again that people succeed most in doing what they love best. If you can accurately determine what you were created by God to do, you will truly find a life you will love living. Here are 4 ways to uncover the calling God has on your life.

1. Delight yourself in the Lord. (Ps. 37:4.) If you take joy in pursuing your personal relationship with Christ each day, the Bible promises that God will put His desires, drive, and passion in your life.

2. Don't be afraid to try new things. Take some risks. Try different kinds of activities, work, and projects. You may find something you're good at that no one knew about, including you.

3. Ask for counsel from people you trust. The Bible says in a multitude of counsel there is safety. (Prov. 11:14.) Ask those close to you with a track record of success what they see you being able to excel at most.

4. Spend regular time in prayer. (Jer. 33:3.) God told Jeremiah that if he would pray and call out to Him, that He would answer him, showing him great and mighty things that he knew not. The Hebrew meaning of that word *mighty* is "hidden."[1] Prayer will unlock things in your life that could have remained hidden forever.

3 Keys to Forecasting the Future

Your plan is always an experiment with the future. A good plan that has any hope of being fulfilled must have accurate forecasting of the future. What field of work will be most valuable to you and others in ten years? What is the next big idea in your area of expertise or interest? If you'll follow these 3 keys, the Lord will help guide you into a successful future others may find dim.

1. Spend time daily in prayer. Jeremiah 33:3 promises that if we call upon the Lord, He will answer us and show us things to come.

2. Remember that history repeats itself. A careful study of history will help us properly anticipate the future. In the early 1900s, people were calling for the U.S. Patent Office to be closed since everything had already been invented and it was unlikely anything new or helpful would come along! This was before airplanes, computers, television, and a million other things. The lesson of this piece of history is to never close your mind to the possibility of change—in any area.

3. Two heads are better than one. I've found that I forecast better when I knock heads with my colleagues or coworkers. Challenge each other to dream and think outside the box called "today."

GOD IS WATCHING

A reality show that made a big hit when it was introduced places fourteen strangers in a house together. These contestants are under the constant surveillance of cameras, and anything they do has the potential of being broadcast on national television. Viewers can also visit the show's Web site to see twenty-four-hour coverage of the group. The object of the game is to see who can last the longest under such strenuous conditions and not be voted off by his or her peers.

One might wonder why a person would subject himself to being in a situation like this, even for the half-million-dollar prize. Yet some people choose to live their entire lives in a similar fashion. They think of God as Someone who is constantly watching their every move, just waiting for them to mess up so He can expose their faults to the world and cast judgment upon them.

God is watching you, but not so He can pick at your faults. He's looking for ways to bless you and to meet your needs.

He's watching out for you to protect you from harm. He delights in you as a parent who watches a young child on a playground giggling and playing carelessly. What He desires more than anything is to have an open, loving relationship with you, His beloved child.

Talk to Him today. Tell Him about your problems and concerns. He wants to help solve them. Tell Him about your hopes and dreams. He wants to make sure they happen. Tell Him about your day. He's interested in every detail and loves just hearing your voice.

First John 4:17-18 TLB gives a beautiful description of the kind of relationship God desires to have with us: "As we live with Christ, our love grows more perfect and complete; so we will not be ashamed and embarrassed at the day of judgment, but can face him with confidence and joy, because he loves us and we love him too. We need have no fear of someone who loves us perfectly; his perfect love for us eliminates all dread of what he might do to us." God doesn't want us to go to Him as cowering waifs waiting to get what's coming to us. Instead, He wants us to approach Him with confidence, as dearly loved children.

So feel the warmth of His embrace as you have a good heart-to-heart with your heavenly Father, your loving Daddy.

3 Secrets to Answered Prayer

If you haven't already, it won't be long before you move out on your own. Actually, you will never be "on your own"—God will always be with you. While you may not have a mother or father there for you all the time, the Lord will be your Provider. The answers you need in every area of life are just a prayer away. Here are 3 secrets to getting the answers you want.

1. Learn to pray according to God's will. (1 John 5:14.) God has promised to give you anything that He has "willed" to you. His Word is His will. Read the Bible carefully, making note of the promises of provision, guidance, healing, and everything else that belongs to you as a son or daughter of God.

2. Believe that God is a rewarder. (Heb. 11:6.) God tells us when we approach Him we should do so believing not only that He is alive, but that He is ready to reward you when you seek Him. God is a good God and has good things for you. Expect His best every day!

3. Stand in faith, even when things don't seem to change. (Heb. 11:17.) Faith believes you have the answers to your prayers even before you see them with your own eyes. After you've prayed for something, begin to thank God that He has heard you and the answer is on the way!

3 Ways to Lift Up a Person Through Prayer

Random prayers, unfounded in Scripture, are a risk at best. Why waste your time praying for something you're not really sure God is going to answer? I believe you can pray confident prayers based on a knowledge of God's will through His Word and get answers. Here are some examples.

1. "The harvest truly is plentiful, but the laborers are few" (Matt. 9:37 NKJV). Pray and ask God to send Christian laborers into the lives of people you are praying will come to the knowledge of the truth.

2. "And I will give you the keys of the kingdom of heaven, and whatever you bind on earth will be bound in heaven, and whatever you loose on earth will be loosed in heaven" (Matt. 16:19 NKJV). You have authority from Jesus to bind up the specific things you see that are trying to deceive and destroy the person you're praying for. You can also loose God's power, love, and even His angels to affect their lives for Christ.

3. "As it is written, 'I have made you a father of many nations,' in the presence of Him whom he believed—God, who gives life to the dead and calls those things which do not exist as though they did" (Rom. 4:17 NKJV). The Bible tells us that we have the faith of God and our spiritual father Abraham. Therefore, we can "call those things that be not as though they were." Call the person you are praying for "saved, serving God, and sold out to kingdom purposes" through the eyes of faith.

5 Scriptures to Pray
Over Your Family

Your family may be entirely Christians, or perhaps you have some who have yet to make Jesus Christ Lord of their lives. Either way, there are several Scriptures that pertain to family that you can begin praying in faith over each one. Here are 5 Scriptures.

1. "And you, fathers, do not provoke your children to wrath, but bring them up in the training and admonition of the Lord" (Eph. 6:4 NKJV). Pray for your mom and dad to have patience in teaching and correcting you in righteousness.

2. "That the God of our Lord Jesus Christ, the Father of glory, may give to you the spirit of wisdom and revelation in the knowledge of Him" (Eph. 1:17 NKJV). Pray that your family members will have God's wisdom and understanding in all their decisions.

3. "And if it seems evil to you to serve the Lord, choose for yourselves this day whom you will serve, whether the gods which your fathers served that were on the other side of the River, or the gods of the Amorites, in whose land you dwell. But as for me and my house, we will serve the Lord" (Josh. 24:15 NKJV). Pray and confess boldly that every person in your household is going to serve the Lord.

4. "So they said, 'Believe on the Lord Jesus Christ, and you will be saved, you and your household'" (Acts 16:31 NKJV). Pray and believe God for the salvation of each member of your family.

5. "The righteous man walks in his integrity; his children are blessed after him" (Prov. 20:7 NKJV). Pray for your parents to walk in truth and integrity, and for the blessing of God to be upon your entire family.

4 Scriptures to Pray Over Your Plan

I believe it is very important to pray the right things over the plan that we make. The Word of God tells us in Proverbs 16:9 NKJV, "A man's heart plans his way, but the Lord directs his steps." We need to take the time to devise a plan, but as we pray, God will direct each and every step to get there. Oftentimes these steps aren't even in our original plan set forth. Here are 4 Scriptures I pray over all my plans.

1. Mark 11:24 NKJV: "Therefore I say to you, whatever things you ask when you pray, believe that you receive them, and you will have them." Believe that you receive your desired goal by faith.

2. Psalm 37:4 NKJV: "Delight yourself also in the Lord, and He shall give you the desires of your heart." Delight yourself in the Lord daily and your desires will be granted.

3. Proverbs 21:5 NKJV: "The plans of the diligent lead surely to plenty, but those of everyone who is hasty, surely to poverty." With diligent work your plan will make you rich.

4. Galatians 6:9 NKJV: "And let us not grow weary while doing good, for in due season we shall reap if we do not lose heart." Have a persevering spirit, knowing that you will reap if you don't give up.

PERMANENT IMMUNITY

On a well-known reality show, contestants are left on an island with minimal food and supplies and must work together to survive the wilderness. One person is voted off the island each week, and the last person standing is awarded a million-dollar prize. Over the course of the thirty-nine days contestants are on the island, strong alliances often form and even some genuine friendships. Yet, in the end, there can be only one winner, so relationships are often abandoned for the all-important prize.

On each episode of the show, contestants have the opportunity to compete in a challenge to earn immunity. The challenges are often painstaking and difficult. Yet contestants pour their all into the competitions, because the person possessing the coveted immunity cannot be voted off the island that week. The winning contestant has the option of giving his or her immunity to another team member, but they must forfeit immunity for themself.

Here's the good news: We all have the opportunity to gain immunity from sin and its consequences. This immunity is called salvation, and it doesn't last for just a week but for all eternity. Even better, we don't even have to do anything to earn it. It's already been purchased for us with the blood that Jesus shed on the cross. It is ours just for the asking.

If that isn't enough, this immunity is limitless. We can share it with as many people as we want without forfeiting our possession of it. In fact, sharing this immunity with others will only strengthen our survival skills here on earth and will earn us priceless rewards in the life to come. After all, what could be better than spending eternity surrounded by those we know and love in a paradise beyond our imaginations. And in that beautiful land, there will be no shortage of food or supplies—only the richest abundance of anything we could ever wish for.

It's time to get busy spreading this permanent immunity. Share it with everyone you know, then get to know others who need this precious gift. Here are some tips on how to get started forming genuine alliances that will have eternal rewards for you and for all those around you.

Reality Check

4 Scriptures That Promise Salvation

It is the Word of God that will speak the strongest to people who need Christ. The Bible says that God watches over His Word to perform it. (Jer. 1:12.) Here are 4 key Scriptures that will arm you with the knowledge you need to present the gospel effectively to any person.

1. "For all have sinned and fall short of the glory of God" (Rom. 3:23 NKJV). People must see that our sin separates us from God.

2. "For the wages of sin is death, but the gift of God is eternal life in Christ Jesus our Lord" (Rom. 6:23 NKJV). People must see that Jesus is the bridge back into relationship with God.

3. "That if you confess with your mouth the Lord Jesus, and believe in your heart that God has raised Him from the dead, you will be saved" (Rom. 10:9 NKJV). People need to see that they must confess Jesus as Lord and Master of their life, believing He rose from the dead in order for them to be saved.

4. "But he who received the seed on stony places, this is he who hears the word and immediately receives it with joy; yet he has no root in himself, but endures only for a while. For when tribulation or persecution arises because of the word, immediately he stumbles" (Matt. 13:20-21 NKJV). People must understand that Satan will try to steal the seed of God's Word that has been planted in their heart. It's up to them to put their roots down deep and resist Satan's lies.

3 Steps to Lead a Person to Christ

Winning people to Christ is one of the easiest things to do if you just know how. I've had the chance to do it hundreds of times. All it really takes is a gentle boldness, and once you do it once, it only gets easier. Here are 3 steps to remember.

1. Cut to the chase and ask. At some point during your conversation with someone about God, stop everything and look them square in the eye and ask, "How would you like to be sure your sins are forgiven and know Jesus as your Lord and Savior?" More times than not, their answer will be, "Sure, I'd like to know that."

2. Stop everything and pray. Don't wait another second. Tell them that they can pray right now and make their heart right with God. You lead the prayer and have them repeat: "Father in heaven, thank You for sending Jesus to die for my sins. I confess Jesus as my Lord and Savior. I believe He is alive and is coming to live in me now. Thank You for forgiving all my sins and giving me a brand-new heart, a heart that wants to please You. In Jesus' name, amen."

3. Do your follow-through. Get them to church. Show them in Scripture the importance of water baptism. Teach them how to read their Bible and pray. They're baby Christians, and you'll have to help them learn to walk.

Reality Check

3 Practical Ways to Show God's Love to a Sinner

Most people who have lost their way in America have heard many a preacher, either in church, on television or radio, or even on the street of their city. They know they have sinned and come short of God's standard. It's going to take more than just more preaching. Jesus preached, but He also showed His love in practical ways. Here are some examples He set for us.

1. Jesus fed the multitude. Why? Because people need food to live and because most people happen to like food! Why not ask a friend who doesn't know Christ out for dinner at a nice restaurant? It's neutral turf. A free meal. It's all good!

2. Jesus healed the sick. The Bible says those who believe will lay hands on the sick and they shall recover. (Mark 16:18 KJV). The next time a friend, family member, or coworker complains about some kind of pain or discomfort, offer to pray for them right there. You are not the healer, but you are inviting the Healer to bring His power into their lives.

3. Jesus washed His disciples' feet. He came to serve, not to be served. What could you do for someone you hope to influence for Christ? Help them in their yard? Clean their car? Assist them with homework? Servanthood is one of the keys that opens the door of the gospel in the lives of people.

4 Do's That Affect Sinners

The Bible encourages us in James 1:22 NKJV to "be doers of the word, and not hearers only." What you say is important, but what you do will give you the right to say it. Here are 4 do's that you must do to influence those around you who do not know Jesus.

1. Do be generous. The Bible says in Proverbs 19:4 that a generous man has many friends. Seek to help meet physical needs of people, and they will eventually trust you with their spiritual needs as well.

2. Do live purely. If you have an immoral lifestyle, your words will fall on deaf ears. Your commitment to have pure relationships with people proves your testimony of a pure relationship with God.

3. Do be real. Have fun. Tell jokes. Enjoy life. Listen to music. Go to good movies. Play practical jokes. You get my drift. Don't try to be so religious that you fail to relate to people. Remember, Jesus was criticized for hanging around sinners, yet He kept Himself separate in His actions.

4. Do be patient. Think about all that God and people put up with in getting your life on track. You do not have the right to give up on anybody!

3 Attitudes That Make You a Hypocrite

Jesus constantly warned people against living a hypocritical life. He knew that hypocrites would cause the greatest damage to the kingdom of God. The word *hypocrite* in the Greek language means to be an actor. Christianity is not a "part" you play on Sunday morning, reverting back to the real you the rest of the week. Beware of these 3 attitudes that every hypocrite has.

1. Being careless. "Who cares what people think about what I do in my personal life? It's none of their business." If you don't care about how your actions affect others, you are on your way to hypocrisy.

2. Being unteachable. "Don't try to tell me what to do or how to live. I will make up my own mind independent of others." This kind of thinking puts you on a dangerous road to ruin. God puts people around us to help guide and protect us. Don't despise their counsel.

3. Comparing. "Well, I'm not as bad as a lot of people I see in the church." This attitude was prevalent in the Pharisees in Jesus' time. These religious hypocrites were always comparing themselves to others who they felt were less spiritual. Their appearances to people were more important than how they appeared to God.

5 Things You Should Know About Sinners

Jesus said in Matthew 4:19 NKJV, "Follow Me, and I will make you fishers of men." Good fishermen study all they can about how to successfully catch fish. They know what kind of bait to use, the right time of day, where in the lake to go, and the proper techniques needed to reel in the big one when it bites onto the hook. We must be just as diligent and wise in our attempts to reach people. Here are 5 things you need to know about sinners.

1. No matter how happy and confident they appear on the outside, deep inside they are empty and searching.

2. When they appear the most stubborn and hard towards your message, they are likely very close to breaking. Don't give up.

3. Their eyes can be opened to truth and the reality of God through your prayers.

4. Most of them already believe in God. They need someone to show them the next step.

5. They are caught better alone than in groups. Try to get with them one-on-one.

3 Reasons Leadership Creates Evangelism

Every person in the world looks for someone else to follow. Someone they can look up to. Someone who's already been where they want to go. If someone like Madonna ever comes to a deep personal faith in Christ, it will likely be a result of someone in her world whom she respects and admires sharing the gospel in a relevant way. Who can God use you to influence as a leader in your world? It may be younger classmates at school or people who look up to you because of a certain talent you have developed. Here are some reasons you can evangelize through leadership.

1. There is a group of people who relate to your interests and respect who you are and what you do. Out of all the people in the world, you have the best possible opportunity to reach them.

2. People everywhere admire risk-takers. That's what a leader does. He or she takes risks by attempting and daring to do things that others stand back and watch.

3. People have trouble arguing with success. They may try to argue with your beliefs, but they cannot argue with the success that your beliefs have produced. The success of Jesus' ministry in healing the sick and raising the dead caused people to listen to His message.

REAL WORLD FRIENDSHIP

As complicated as friendships can seem in high school, they tend to become even more complex after school, in the "real world." Seven strangers from very different backgrounds get a chance to experience this phenomenon firsthand on each season of a popular teen reality show that places them in a house together for three months. They all have their own goals of what they want to accomplish during their time spent in the big city, and each has a different dream to pursue. But they all have to learn how to get along with each other during their time together.

Some are open and ready to make new friends and to learn about the other people in the house. Others are so focused on their own goal that they estrange themselves from everyone. To some, the only relationships worth spending time on are the ones that will take them closer to what they want to gain from the time. Still others tend to put up a guard against everyone in the house out of a fear of being hurt.

As you go out into the world to make a life for yourself, how will friendship rank in your list of priorities? In the midst of building a career for yourself and exploring your interests, it can be easy to let relationships slide and not give them the attention they deserve. If you've never experienced the joy of having a truly great friendship, in which each person is more concerned about the other person's happiness than his or her own, you may not view friendship as being very important.

But God's Word places great value on friendship. In Matthew 22:37-40, Jesus simplifies the entire contents of the Bible into two very important commandments: Love God and love other people. If loving other people is one of the top two reasons we've been placed on this earth, friendship must be a pretty big deal to God.

After all, what is there besides our relationships that we can take with us into eternity? We can't take our money, our car, our house, or even our list of accomplishments, but we can take our friends. Matthew 6:19-20 talks about storing up treasures in heaven. When you think of your friends as eternal treasures, they're sure to move up a few spaces on your priority list.

6 Keys to Getting Along With a Roommate

Most people will have at least one roommate in life, and if you don't, you will most likely get married and live with your spouse. So, here are some good tips to getting along with your roommate or spouse.

1. Establish the house rules. Most arguments that occur are misunderstandings because the rules were not clearly defined. So sit down together and write out the rules of the house. What are the rules about picking up after yourself, bringing guests over, cooking meals, the groceries, and the volume of the TV late at night.

2. Respect each other's stuff. Most fights that occur are the result of not respecting each other's personal belongings or space. Don't use your roommate's new sweater without permission or drink their last can of Coke. Remember the golden rule of having a roommate and you will eliminate many arguments: "Do unto your roommate's stuff as you would have them do unto yours."

3. Don't let your frustrations build up. Jesus teaches us in Matthew to talk to those who offend us. (Matt. 18:15.) Rather than letting it build up or gossip to others about it, we must work it out with the person who offends us. Most of the time it was a simple misunderstanding and your relationship will become stronger because you dealt with it. Relationships take work, lots of work, but they are worth it.

4. Prefer them above yourself. Paul wrote to the Philippians that we are to be like Christ and prefer others above ourselves. (Phil. 2:3-5.) Don't always think about what you want. Stop and think about the needs of your roommate and put them above your own. If you do this you will be amazed to see the difference it will make in the way your roommate treats you. According to Galatians 6:7, whatever a man sows, that is what he will reap.

5. Don't focus on the little things. It is amazing how most arguments happen over little things that make no difference in eternity, or even in this life for that matter. Stop, take a step back, and ask yourself if this will really matter a month from now or even at the end of the day.

6. Give them space for themselves. Everyone needs time to be alone. Respect your roommate's need for privacy. Before you have guests come over, call and see if it is okay. Little gestures of thoughtfulness like this will go a long way to building lasting friendships you can enjoy for years to come.

5 Surefire Ways to Make New Friends in a New Place

A new place can often be intimidating and lonely. But it can also be a great adventure if you take the initiative to meet new people. Even if you are naturally a shy person, if you follow these simple steps you will find it easy to make new friends.

1. Take advantage of every opportunity to introduce yourself to people. Introduce yourself to people in the school bookstore, cafeteria, library, and in class. The more people you meet the greater the odds you will find people you really connect with.

2. Remember to use people's names. There is no better sound to a person than his or her own name. If you aren't good at remembering names, here is a little trick that will help. When you introduce yourself and your new acquaintance gives you their name, be sure to use it right away. For example, "Fred, it sure is good to meet you. Fred, what classes do you have this semester?" If you can use their name at least three times in your conversation you will be more likely to remember their name. They will also be impressed the next time you see them and use their name.

3. Ask them questions about themselves. Your conversation will be a hit because you are talking about their favorite subject— them! Everyone's favorite subject is themselves. It is often said, God gave us two ears and one mouth because He wants us to do twice as much listening as talking. A university study has found that good listening can be worth as much as 20 IQ points. I'll take all the extra points I can get!

4. Have good eye contact. If your eyes are always wandering during your conversation, people will feel you are uninterested in them. Also, poor eye contact can send them the message you are insecure or you are hiding something from them.

5. Be selective when choosing your closest friends. Close friends are people who influence your values, self-esteem, and dreams. Be careful to choose friends who love God as you do, believe in your dreams, and build you up. If they are always tearing you down, you can do something about it—get some new friends. A famous mathematician once said, "You have to have seven positives to overcome one negative." Life is too short to waste it with people who don't believe in you.

5 Ways to Attract New Friends

Lee Iacocca says, "Success comes not from what you know, but from who you know and how you present yourself to each of those people."[2] Good friendships are vital to success. Maybe you are in need of some good friends.

Here are 5 ways to attract new friends.

1. Smile. Turn that frown upside down. This gesture may be small, but it packs a powerful punch. Showing those pearly whites is a magnet to new friends (be sure those pearls are white). (Prov. 18:24.)

2. Listen. Let others talk about themselves, then respond. When someone else is talking, don't be thinking about what you're going to say. Give the person your ear before expressing your thoughts. (Prov. 17:28.)

3. Be dependable. Be there for others during the good and the bad. Anyone can be there for the fun times, but only a friend will be there when things get rough.

4. Keep your word. If you say you are going to do something, do it. Keep your word even if you don't feel like it. If you can't keep a promise, then don't make it. It's better to under-promise and overachieve. (Prov. 11:3.)

5. Help others succeed. Be others-minded. Ask yourself, "How can I help this person?" Then do something about it. If you have this mind-set, you will attract so many friends you won't know what to do.

5 Questions Real Friends Should Ask Each Other

A smart person is known by the good questions he or she asks. When Jesus was 12 years old, He was found in the temple asking questions of the teachers of the law.

Here are 5 questions that good friends should ask each other.

1. How can I be a better friend to you?

2. Are there any traits, attitudes, or actions you see in my life that hinder my success?

3. What gifts and characteristics do you recognize as strengths in my life?

4. How can I pray for you at this time in your life?

5. What has God shown you in His Word lately?

Reality Check

4 Steps to Building Strong Relationships With the Friends You Already Have

Sometimes the hardest relationships to develop are the ones you have for a long time. It can be easy to take them for granted because it seems like those people will simply be there forever. Those people that you are closest to will be the biggest influence on your life, so developing these relationships is critical to your future. Here are 4 steps that you can take to make those relationships stronger.

1. Be the kind of friend you want. Sitting around wishing that your friends would treat you better is only going to wear out the couch. Start treating your friends the way you want them to treat you, and you will begin to see them treat you the same way. (Matt. 7:12.)

2. Ask questions. Be proactive. Find out how your friends are doing. Ask them about the things that they are involved in. Focus the questions on things you know they talk about, and be prepared to listen or help.

3. Offer your help when needed. No one likes to ask for help; offering your assistance will go a long way with your friends. A strong friendship means being ready to lend a hand to the projects and needs of others without making them beg or feel like they owe you a huge debt.

4. Be an encouragement. Try to be as supportive as possible of your friend's ideas or ambitions. You don't have to support

dangerous or immoral ideas, but when it's within reason, offer your support. Don't be too quick to laugh or criticize; try always to be your friend's biggest cheerleader.

4 Steps to Finding Favor With Friends

Everyone wants to have good friends. In order to have a good friend, you must learn to be one. There are very real reasons why everyone seems to like some people, while others are constantly rejected. Here are 4 practical steps to finding good friends.

1. Break out of your shell of fear. Don't wait for people to reach out to you. Be bold to say hello to people and make conversation.

2. Give friends their space. Don't monopolize people's time or constantly follow them around. When you begin to smother people with attention, they will naturally want to avoid you.

3. Be confident in yourself and your abilities. If you are constantly putting yourself down and wallowing in self-pity, people will tire of you soon.

4. Have a giving heart without trying to "buy" your friendships. Be generous and thoughtful without feeling like you have to do things to keep a certain friend. If you have to buy or give someone something all the time, the person is probably not a friend anyway.

7 Bible Guarantees
for Friendship

God recognized man's need for relationship when He created a companion for Adam in the Garden of Eden. In Genesis 2:18 NKJV, God said, "It is not good that man should be alone." We need godly relationships in our lives to strengthen and encourage us. Here are 7 Bible guarantees for friendship.

1. God's Word guarantees that you will have friends if you show yourself friendly. Proverbs 18:24 NKJV says, "A man who has friends must himself be friendly." The Bible encourages you to take the first step and initiate friendships. You will have quality friends if you make the effort to always be friendly.

2. God's Word guarantees that godly friends make you stronger. Proverbs 27:17 NKJV says, "As iron sharpens iron, so a man sharpens the countenance of his friend." As you grow in your relationship with God and pursue godly relationships, the friends you choose to surround yourself with will either move you closer to or further away from your goals. Good friends will sharpen you, because they are moving in the same direction as you.

3. God's Word guarantees that godly friends will help you realize your potential. Proverbs 20:5 NKJV says, "Counsel in the heart of man is like deep water, but a man of understanding will draw it out." God has a unique purpose for you. Good friendships will help you achieve all that God has planned for your future.

4. God's Word guarantees that true friends will stick with you no matter what. Proverbs 17:17 NKJV says, "A friend loves at all

times, and a brother is born for adversity." Fair-weather friends will leave at the first sign of trouble. But true friends do not change their attitude towards you just because negative circumstances arise.

5. God's Word guarantees that you will become wise if you hang out with wise friends. Proverbs 13:20 NKJV says, "He who walks with wise men will be wise...." Friendships influence almost all of our choices. Surround yourself with wise friends who can help you make wise choices in every area of life.

6. God's Word guarantees that you can avoid suffering by not hanging out with foolish people. Proverbs 13:20 NKJV says, "...But the companion of fools will be destroyed." This verse warns that if you choose to hang out with foolish friends, you will share the same fate they have. So choose to avoid inevitable heartache by steering clear of those who make bad choices.

7. God's Word guarantees that you will reap what you sow into your friendships. Galatians 6:7 NKJV says, "...whatever a man sows, that he will also reap." If you spend time developing strong relationships, those relationships can become a great resource. Friendships have to be nurtured in order to thrive. If you take your friends for granted, the relationships will eventually wither and die.

5 Attitudes That Are Friend Magnets

There are always those people who you are naturally attracted to, those friends who you want to spend all of your free time with. What is it about those people that makes others want to be around them? Here are 5 character traits that make people friend magnets.

1. Happiness. Nobody wants to be around a grump. A great attitude is one of the strongest magnets for friends. When you are happy, it's contagious. Always try to stay upbeat, and you will never cease to be in the company of friends.

2. Encouraging. Choosing to lift other people up with a kind word or a generous action will naturally draw other people to your side. A word in due season is often just the encouragement someone else needs. (Prov. 15:23 NKJV.)

3. Generosity. Unselfishness has a powerfully attractive force. By choosing to share and think of others before yourself, you show people that you value them.

4. Objective. It's nice to be around people who are willing to hear the opinions of others. Let's face it, you're not always right, so pick your battles carefully and be willing to accept someone else's idea if it's better than yours.

5. Helpfulness. You're not much of a friend if you're not willing to lend a hand. It works both ways. There will be a time when you need some help, so sow the seeds of friendship now, and you will reap the rewards later.

4 Ways to Make a Relationship "Win-Win"

Being involved in a relationship that is one-sided can be incredibly frustrating. You don't want to be constantly giving and giving without receiving anything from that relationship yourself. Every healthy relationship is mutually beneficial; it is good for both sides. These are 4 ways to make every relationship a "win-win."

1. Start with you. The best way to ensure that your relationships are not one-sided is to avoid the things that drain your friendships. Make sure that you are not being selfish or self-centered. Begin to look to do things for others before you expect things to be done for you.

2. Know your limits. Decide ahead of time what you are willing to do and what you are not. If you know your limits and what your priorities are, you will avoid getting into situations where you feel that your friends have taken advantage of you.

3. Be willing to say "no." Just because you say "no" to certain things doesn't mean that you are saying "no" to the whole relationship. The sooner you decide that you cannot do everything for everyone, the sooner you can relax and trust that kindly saying "no" will allow you to do the things that are important to you and avoid the things that waste your time.

4. Be quick to say "yes." Saying "no" to certain things will help you manage your time, but that doesn't mean that in a healthy relationship you never say "yes." In order to develop a good relationship you must be quick to say "yes" when you are able to or when others have a need.

3 Secrets to Making New Friends

Everyone wants to be liked. That is no different in the "work world." People want friends and they want to be friendly, even those who seem a little "stuck up." Networking is really just the process of meeting new people and making new friends. People are your best resource as you work toward your career, so here are 3 secrets that will help you network and make new friends.

1. Be friendly. It seems obvious, but many people get so focused on the task in front of them that they miss the people and possible relationships passing them by. Grab each opportunity to build new relationships by doing the small things that make it happen. Say hello, introduce yourself, or simply smile. Make the first effort by showing yourself friendly. (Prov. 18:24 KJV.)

2. Focus on others. People want to talk about things that matter to them. If you spend 4 hours talking about your last doctor's appointment to someone you just met, don't be surprised if they start avoiding you. Make the effort to find out what they like and focus on things that you have in common.

3. Do kind things without looking for credit. The simple principle of sowing and reaping works in friendships too. If you begin to go out of your way to sow into the lives of people, you will begin to reap the kind of friends that you want. (Gal. 6:7.)

3 Friendship Killers You Must Avoid

Good friends are hard to come by, and acquiring good friends is only half the battle. The other half is keeping them. If you want to keep your friends, I suggest you don't do these friendship killers.

1. Gossip. Gossip is simply mischievous talk about the affairs of others. Proverbs 16:28 says that a gossip separates close friends. A good friend will keep what he or she knows in confidence, unless someone in authority needs to be notified.

2. Selfishness. How can we expect to keep the company of others if we are concerned only about ourselves? In Philippians 2:3, Paul wrote that we are to consider others better than ourselves. If we act unselfishly, we will encourage our friendships to grow.

3. Unforgiveness. Our friends will make mistakes. Why? Because they are human. As our friends miss it and then turn from their mistakes or sin, we are to forgive them. We are to forgive our friends as Christ forgave us. (Eph. 4:31-32.)

PARENTS JUST DON'T UNDERSTAND

A show that had its beginnings in the U.K. and is now attracting large audiences in the U.S. and other countries stars a nanny who has over sixteen years' experience in raising children. Viewers are attracted to the show because of the nanny's practical advice and creative ideas about how to produce a loving environment that will foster good behavior in children. Many of the families she helps are in desperate need of some change. Yelling matches, temper tantrums, and a total loss of control and order are their normal modes of operation.

The nanny works with the children some, but her main focus is on changing the parents' behavior. She realizes that children will imitate the behavior of their parents. When parents yell and don't have control of themselves, the children yell, act out in anger, and are out of control. Likewise, if the parents are calm and controlled, the children calm down and are more controlled. So if the nanny can change the parents' behavior, the children's behavior improves drastically too. The transformations that occur on each episode are quite amazing, and viewers get the privilege of seeing hope renewed in what seemed like a hopeless situation.

What is your home life like? Could your family use some advice from an experienced nanny? The teen years can be a tough time for you and your parents, especially if communication isn't the greatest. You're developing ideas of your own about how you want to live your life, but your parents still have a responsibility to protect you and to do what they think is right for you. Maybe you desire a close relationship with your parents, but you come from a broken home or one or both parents haven't been the greatest examples for you.

Whatever your situation, God has a solution. There is hope for your relationship with your parents. Ephesians 5:1 tells us to "be imitators of God, therefore, as dearly loved children." This means that even if our parents are the exact opposites of who we want to be, we aren't left without a clue of how we should live. We have our heavenly Father, the best example we could ever follow. And it gets even better. If you will begin to imitate your Father in heaven, the nanny's ideas for modifying the behavior of children will also work in reverse. If your communication with your parents is calm and controlled, it will have a calming effect on your parents. If you act in a more reasonable, respectful fashion, your parents will tend to be more respectful of your ideas and communicate more reasonably with you.

As the families on the show experience, changes in family relations take time and require a great deal of patience. But the mended relationships are well worth the effort.

3 Steps to Finding Favor With Your Parents

One of the coolest things in life is enjoying a happy home. You can learn to become a source of joy in your family. I've got 3 teenage boys who everyone at school and church thinks are really "cool." But they are also great guys at home. The rebel attitude is not cool. In fact, it will cause you some very "uncool" moments in life. Here are 3 things you can do to ensure a great time at home.

1. Choose to obey your parents immediately, whether you feel like it or not. You're eventually going to have to do it—right? So just get it done and out of the way.

2. Honor your parents when you speak to them. Even if you don't agree with them and want to discuss something or negotiate a "better deal," do it without the anger and the attitude. You'll be amazed at the results!

3. Be truthful, even when it gets you in trouble. You lose favor quickly when you cannot be trusted. It is better to take the heat if you have it coming than to lie and avoid it. Lies are eventually uncovered, and the consequences are much more damaging than telling the truth would have been.

3 Marks of a Proud Parent

I don't know that I've ever met a teenager who didn't want their parents to be proud of them. There's no one who knows you better than your mom and dad. If you can make them proud of your character and accomplishments, well done! Here are 3 goals to aspire to as a son or daughter.

1. They look forward to taking you out in public. It may be a restaurant, an event, or something else, but proud parents look for opportunities to spend extra time with you and show the world what a great kid they have.

2. You become the topic of every conversation (and not because of trouble you've gotten into). Proud parents can't wait to brag on you to their friends and neighbors. They've had a part in seeing you grow up and are thrilled to see you succeed.

3. They want to help you fulfill your dreams. When you've worked hard to please Mom and Dad, their natural desire will be to do anything in their ability to assist you in reaching your goals in life.

Reality Check

3 Ways to Deal With Tough Parents

Parents aren't perfect. I know this because I am one. I've made mistakes in raising my kids, and I am the first to admit it to them when I've missed the mark. Even so, there are some parents who are really tough to deal with and are perhaps too hard on their kids. Here are some ways to handle parents who may be extremely difficult to get along with.

1. Practice a soft answer. The Bible says that a soft answer turns away wrath and anger. (Prov. 15:1 NKJV.) Learn to hold your tongue and your temper, even when a parent does not. Do your best to set an example of patience and gentleness.

2. Communicate well. Be sure that you never leave a parent in the dark about what you're doing, where you're going, or when you're planning to do something. Practice the "no surprise" rule. And learn to ask, rather than tell or demand. Give them the satisfaction of granting you permission, even on things you may take for granted.

3. Don't become a victim of physical abuse. If you have a parent who has become violent, constantly hitting you or beating you up physically, please let someone know who can help you. (I'm not talking about getting spankings while growing up.) Get help from a family member you trust or perhaps a church pastor or school counselor.

4 Ways to Tell Parents "Thank You"

I believe one of the greatest character traits that you can develop in your life is appreciation and gratefulness towards others. It's important that you find practical ways to show gratitude to someone who has been a blessing to you. Nothing warms my heart more as a father than when one of my boys takes the time to tell Cathy and me thanks for something we've done for them. Here are some ways you can say thanks.

1. A card. Take the time to write out your feelings towards your parents, accounting for the specific things they've done that you are grateful for.

2. A gift. It doesn't have to be expensive. Maybe it's a gift certificate to their favorite restaurant or store. A small sacrifice of finances on your part communicates a big message to Mom and Dad.

3. Unexpected work. Do something around the house you weren't asked to do: the trash, the dishes, the yard—whatever. Tell them you just wanted to find a way to say thanks.

4. Go ahead and tell them. Say it out loud and say it whenever they've done something good for you. A good meal. Permission to use the car. A night at the movies. Tell them thanks!

Reality Check

3 Reasons to Help Your Parents

It's your parents' house, right? It's their yard, their dishes, their cars and windows and carpet. So why should kids have to work on all this stuff? After all, what are children anyway—free labor?! Aren't there laws against this? The truth is, you use all this stuff too, and there are 3 reasons you owe it to Mom and Dad to help take care of it.

1. Good parents have a responsibility to teach their child how to work. If you hope to succeed in life on your own, you're going to have to know how to get a job done right. Parents will be the best bosses you'll ever have!

2. Your help around the house is a small return on a huge investment these people have made in your life: childbirth, diaper changing, late-night bottle feedings, trips to the zoo, vacations, free food, clothes, entertainment, and schooling (they pay taxes for that). I could go on, but you get it!

3. Because Jesus told us to. In Matthew 5:41, He said that if someone asks you to go one mile for them, offer to go two. Our willingness to help others in a practical way is a testimony of God's goodness in our lives towards them.

3 Ways Helping Your Parents Helps You

"What do I get out of this?" I'm glad you asked. Perhaps you get an allowance that you can point to as some form of payment for your help with the family chores. But maybe not. We've never had a regular allowance with any of our teenagers, but they've always worked very willingly because they care about our family and understand that rewards will come. So here are 3 ways helping out Mom and Dad will help you even more.

1. Welcome to training camp for life's big leagues. I'm so glad now that my parents instilled great work habits in me when I was a teenager. They gave me all that I would need to make my bosses happy and get me many raises along the way.

2. You are sowing seed that will harvest in your own home one day. I believe one of the reasons my 3 boys have always been good workers in our home is that I was a good worker in my house. The Bible says in Galatians that God is never mocked and that anytime a seed of any kind is sown, you will reap in due season. (vv. 6:7,9 NKJV.)

3. Helping Mom and Dad gives you favor with them. It won't be long until you really need something from your parents. Every willing, well-done work puts another good deposit into your favor account with them. Withdrawals are easier when you've put something into the bank.

Reality Check

3 Things You Must Tell Your Parents

Communication is the key to victory in any kind of relationship. Great companies, great armies, great churches, great sports teams, and great homes all have one thing in common: They have learned to communicate effectively with one another. Communication is not just talking. It is listening, observing, studying, and finally, talking. People who only learn to talk are not communicating; they are spewing. In opening up good communication lines with your parents, there are 3 things you must always tell them.

1. Tell them when you need help. It may be in school, a relationship, or a job, but if you need help and guidance, let your parents know. That's why God gave them to you—to help you get through tough times.

2. Tell them when you've made a mistake. It might be easier at the time to try to cover it up, but honesty will not only help you to not make this same mistake again, it will also earn you big points in the "trust" quest.

3. Tell them you love and appreciate them. Sure, there's no such thing as a perfect parent, but most all of them have made a very significant investment of time, energy, and money in their children. Regularly let them know you love them, even if they don't always show the same love in return.

2 Things Never to Tell Your Parents

My wife, Cathy, and I have had the privilege of raising 3 wonderful boys, who, at the writing of this book, are all teenagers, and one has graduated. They have not been fault-less and neither have we, but in spite of the challenges that come in any family, we are very, very close to them. All 3 of my sons would honestly say that Dad is their best friend. To their credit, there are 2 things they have never told me—and you shouldn't tell your parents these things either.

1. Never tell your parents you hate them. You may disagree, be annoyed, or become a little irritated, but the word *hate* is a terrible word that can break the spirit and will of the strongest person. Take it out of your vocabulary, except when talking about sin and the devil.

2. Never tell your parents you wish you hadn't been born. Maybe life has been hard. Perhaps you haven't had the breaks that other kids in your school have enjoyed. But remember this: God created you, and He made you for a purpose. Oftentimes, kids who rise above a difficult upbringing become a great success because of things they learned.

7 Questions to Ask Your Parents in the Next 7 Days

Asking questions is a great way to learn and grow. You gain a perspective on areas of your life that you may have never realized. Here are 7 questions to ask your parents in the next 7 days. Learn from each answer.

1. How can I be a better son or daughter?

2. What do you see as my greatest strengths?

3. What do you think are the weaknesses that I must work on?

4. What friends do you see as the best influences in my life?

5. What kind of career could you see me getting into after I graduate?

6. When do I make you most proud?

7. What is the most important thing you've learned in life?

7 Things a Parent Loves in a Teenager

The Bible tells us that a wise child will make one's father happy, but a foolish child will cause one's mother grief. (Prov. 10:1.) The attitudes and actions you display in your home have a major influence on the happiness of your family.

Here are 7 things you can do to bring joy in your family.

1. Do your chores without someone asking you to do them.

2. Offer to help with something around the house that is not usually your responsibility.

3. Think of a compliment you can give your mom, dad, or both.

4. Ask your parents if there is anything you can do to improve your behavior.

5. When asked to do something, don't procrastinate even a minute—go right to it.

6. If you have a brother or sister, treat your sibling with the same respect that you would want in return.

7. Be polite, thoughtful, and helpful outside of your home, at school, and in other activities.

3 Reasons Your Relationship With Your Parents Will Affect Your Career

Your relationship with your parents is simply preparation for the rest of your life, including your work and career. There are at least 3 important reasons your career will either succeed or fail as a direct result of how you get along with the authority in your home.

1. If you can't honor and obey those who love you in your home, it's unlikely you'll behave any better with a boss who won't be nearly as likely to forgive. Remember, your parents will be the last bosses you have who can't fire you.

2. Your parents have already been where you are headed. They have experienced the real world. If you're smart, you'll ask questions, listen to their experiences and wisdom, and learn what it takes to succeed.

3. There will be times when school, chores, and life at home will seem boring and redundant. The day will come when you will experience the same feelings with your job and career. Learning to persevere and rejuvenate your passion will put you ahead of the pack.

Reality Check

FRIENDS THROUGH THICK AND THIN

Sometimes the best words you can say to your friend are those he or she least wants to hear. It isn't easy to confront a friend about a problem in his or her life. One reality show attempts to make this process easier by providing a counselor who arranges an intervention. At the intervention, friends and family of the person being confronted gather together to deliver their messages of tough love and to ask the person to seek help. The problem being addressed might be alcoholism, smoking, a drug addiction, abusive tendencies toward a spouse or children, or an addiction to gambling. Whatever the problem, words never come easily, and many tears are shed. Yet in the end, the person is usually much better off for having been made to face the issue and deal with it, and relationships are restored.

Do you have a friend who is dealing with some serious problems? It can be intimidating to think about confronting him or her about the issue. You may be afraid that your friend won't like you anymore. Perhaps it's easier to just stop hanging out with that person so you don't become part of the wrong crowd. If you're having trouble resisting the temptation to become involved in the same bad things your friend is doing, by all means, remove yourself from the situation. But let your friend know why you can't hang out any longer. That might be the catalyst needed to get your friend thinking about his or her actions.

Proverbs 27:10 says, "Do not forsake your friend." If your friend is open to seeking help, let him or her know you'll be there all the way; then make sure you are. Help your friend go to his or her parents with the problem if possible. If that's not a plausible solution, help your friend find a professional counselor or youth pastor he or she can trust. You most likely won't be able to solve your friend's problems on your own, but you can help your friend get headed down the path to recovery and restoration.

More than anything, your friend needs to know about the intervention Christ made on our behalf. Tell your friend about Jesus' sacrifice for us, about His love and forgiveness for every kind of sinner. Let him or her see that love and forgiveness in you.

4 Reasons It's Critical That You Listen to People

Many times, the best preaching and teaching that Christ did was a direct result of listening to someone. People would come to Him with sometimes simple and other times very difficult questions. The Holy Spirit would give Jesus the answer every time. James 1:19 tells us to "be quick to listen, slow to speak." A listening heart attracts many friends and will always be rewarded with wisdom from heaven. Here are 4 reasons to have a listening heart.

1. Listening gives you time to fully evaluate a person's situation before you pass on counsel or advice that is premature.

2. Listening tells the person you care. It says that person is important and you are not in a rush to get them down the road.

3. Listening gives you time to hear from God. The Lord will speak to you clearly when you take unselfish interest in the lives of others.

4. God believes in listening. What do you think He's doing when we pray? That's why He gave us 2 ears and 1 mouth. We ought to listen twice as much as we talk.

3 Secrets of a Good Listener

The Bible says in James 1:19 that we are to "be quick to listen, slow to speak." Unfortunately, many people are just the opposite and are very quick to speak and extremely slow to listen. When you take the time to listen to somebody, you are showing them that you care and have respect for what they think. It will cement your relationship with that person. What does it take to be a good listener? Here are 3 secrets.

1. Look into the eyes of the person you are listening to. This, more than anything, says, "I really do care about what you have to say."

2. Think about the point or concern they are making. Don't be rehearsing in your mind your answer before you've fully caught all that they are communicating.

3. Repeat back a brief synopsis of what they just told you. For example, "Jim, I understand that you want to borrow $150 from me, but number one, I'm not a bank, and number two, I don't have an extra $150."

3 Messages That Lift People Up

We grow up in a down world. Comedian Jerry Seinfeld pokes fun of parents who are always using the word *down* with their children. "Get down!" "Settle down." "Quiet down." "Turn that thing down!" You get the point. Many of the messages people hear in our world are not very positive. The nightly news is full of stories of war, crime, and tragedy. When you have a message of something that encourages, you are sure to stand out from the crowd. Here are 3 messages you can share that will lift a person up.

1. "God created you to succeed in life." But like any created thing, you must find out exactly what you were created to do. A hammer isn't very good at being a screwdriver. But it's powerful when used for its creative purpose.

2. "No matter what you've done, Jesus Christ loves you without conditions." The Bible says that while we were yet sinners, Christ died for us. (Rom. 5:8 KJV.) When we were at our worst, Jesus gave us His very best.

3. "Heaven is a little like earth, without the bad days." The Bible talks about streets, trees, and rivers in heaven. So there are similarities to earth. Yet it promises no pain and no tears! It is absent of tragedy, depression, and temptation. And God has a mansion prepared for every one of His children. (John 14:2; Rev. 21:4, 21; 22:1- 2.)

7 Ways to Help a Suicidal Person

Believe it or not, there are people you know and meet every day who battle severe discouragement and depression. Some even feel like the life they have isn't worth living. Given the opportunity, God can use each of us to help a discouraged soul find purpose and meaning that will create a future worth living for. Here are some ways you can help a person who seems to have lost the will to go on.

1. Never treat talk or hints of suicide lightly. Whether they are actually serious or not, any discussion of ending life deserves serious and immediate attention.

2. Do not leave this person alone. You stay with them until they are back in the care of their family or guardian.

3. Encourage them from the Word of God. Jeremiah 29:11 promises them a future if they will put their trust in Christ.

4. Pray with them for God to intervene, and allow Him to give you the words to say at the end of your prayer.

5. Help them find pastoral counsel and/or a professional Christian counselor to help them learn to overcome depression.

6. Be sure that they have no access to any weapons or opportunities to hurt themselves.

7. Provide regular follow-up in your friendship, supplying them with tapes, books, and other encouraging material.

3 Things to Say to a Victim of Divorce

According to national statistics, nearly half of all marriages in America have their last words in a court of law. The divorce court—a place where two people give up. Oftentimes, those who are hurt the most had nothing to do with the marriage in the first place. Children of divorced parents are forced to deal with a lot of very adult issues at a young age. Here are 3 things you can say to help.

1. **"Anytime you need to vent, I'm here."** Often a person just needs to talk things out and needs someone like you to listen. Sure, God will use you to provide wisdom and encouragement, but an attentive ear may be the most important gift you can give.

2. **"Unforgiveness is a choice to hurt yourself even more."** As much as you don't feel like it, you must make the decision to forgive your parents. Not forgiving them only builds up the poison of bitterness and resentment that will infect all of your other relationships. For your own sake, forgive and begin to move on to all that God has for you.

3. **"None of this is your fault."** Parents have the power to make the right choices in life and have no one to blame but themselves for their decisions. Although feelings of guilt will try to attach themselves to you, resist each and every one—they don't belong to you!

5 Things an Addict Needs to Know

Whether it's street drugs, script pills, alcohol, or sniffing glue, what may begin as a really great high can, over a short period of time, become a terribly destructive addiction. Addiction sneaks up on its victims like a ghost in the night. The costs are enormous: family, friends, career, money, and finally, life. So where do you start in trying to help someone who's hooked? Here is a good place to start.

1. God promises them a way out if they'll commit to do their part. (2 Cor. 10:4.)

2. They can't possibly do it alone. It may be a 12-step program or a church recovery group, but they will need the support of friends and professional help.

3. Cravings, in most cases, won't leave overnight, but will draw down when battled consistently over time until victory is complete. They didn't become an addict overnight, and freedom will demand a fight.

4. They must replace old thought patterns that got them into trouble with Scripture from the Word of God that has been memorized and quoted daily. Even Jesus resisted Satan by speaking the Word of God. (Matt. 4:10.)

5. If they stumble along the road of recovery, get up, dust off, and keep walking towards their freedom. They may not have immediate perfection, but they must have indomitable persistence.

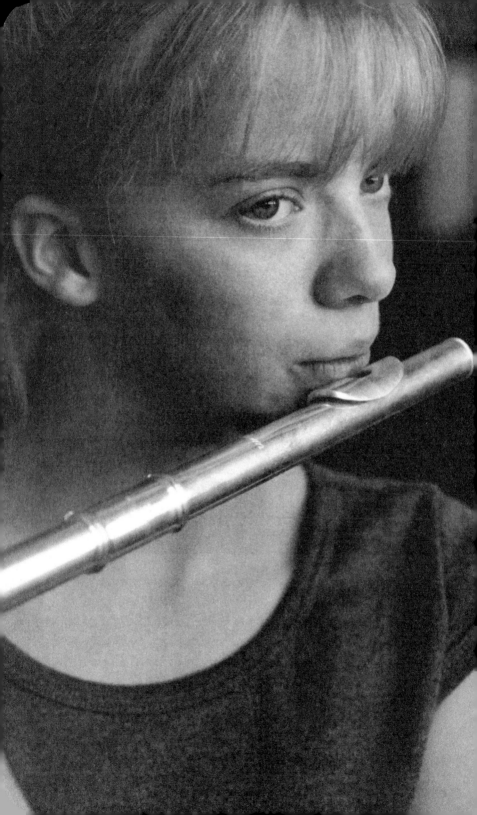

GOD-MADE

Is there something you want to do that seems out of your reach at the moment? Are there ideals you have for yourself that, try as you may, you just can't quite seem to live up to? What is it you want to do more that anything else?

A certain show aims to help teenagers realize their biggest dreams, things that have previously seemed unattainable to them. One episode might feature a girl who has always wanted to be a cheerleader but never had the opportunity to take dance classes and is somewhat overweight. Another episode might be about a guy with less-than-perfect social skills who is considered to be a bit of a computer geek but desperately wants to go out on a date. Those who are chosen to be on the show are given six weeks and a personal trainer to help them achieve their goals. Viewers watch as these teens are pushed to their limits. They often get discouraged and are sometimes close to quitting, but when they stick with their goals to the end, they all come away better for it.

What are your goals? Are you working toward achieving them, or have you let discouragement keep you from moving forward? Maybe you've never really put much thought into your goals, or maybe there are so many things you'd like to do, you're not sure where to start.

When you consider setting a goal for yourself, first take a look at the motive behind it. Sometimes, goals can be motivated by selfishness; these goals probably aren't worth the effort required to fulfill them. But most often, God has placed those desires in your heart for a reason. Maybe He has something great He wants to do through you, and He's just waiting for you to get past your fear and step into His plan.

After you've decided on a goal, count the cost. Be honest with yourself about the work you'll need to put into achieving your goal. It likely won't be easy; most things that are truly worth doing take effort. But if this desire won't let you rest until you achieve it, then it's well worth the effort you'll put into making it happen.

Finally, realize that nothing is impossible with God. Don't talk yourself out of following your dream because you think it's too big or difficult for you to accomplish. God doesn't often place dreams in our hearts that we're able to achieve without His help. That's because He wants us to depend on Him and to see His power at work rather than getting caught up in ourselves and how great we are. When the time comes, God will give you what you need to succeed.

So decide on a goal, drop the excuses, and go for it! God will make you a success.

4 Surefire Ways to Discover Your Talents

Proverbs 18:16 NKJV says, "A man's gift makes room for him, and brings him before great men." The discovery and implementation of your gifts and talents will bring you the success your heart desires.

Here are 4 ways to uncover your talents.

1. Ask those you know and trust what they see as your greatest talents.

2. Pray and ask God to reveal your gifts and talents to you. Jeremiah 33:3 AMP promises that if we call on God, He'll show us hidden things which we don't know about.

3. Follow your heart's desires, and try new things. The results may surprise you.

4. Be faithful in little things you're asked to do, even if they aren't on your list of favorites. God tells us that if we're faithful in small things, we will be rulers over much. (Matt. 25:23.)

3 Keys to Effective Planning

If you want success, you must plan for it. Someone once asked Wayne Gretzky how he became the best goal scorer in the history of hockey. He replied, "While everyone else is chasing the puck, I go to where the puck is going to be." He planned ahead. Let's take a look at 3 keys to effective planning.

1. Prayer. You may not know what the future holds, but God does. God promises that if you will ask Him, He will show you things that you could never figure out on your own. (Jer. 33:3.)

2. Goal setting. Write out exactly what it is you are planning for. You will be amazed how this key will unlock your future.

3. Prioritizing. You can't keep your priorities if you don't have any. Putting things in order will help you plan for and accomplish the most important things first.

8 Goals to Reach Before You're 18

At every stage in life, it is important to learn to set incremental goals towards the fulfillment of your dreams and vision. I encourage you to write down your goals as a regular reference point for your progress. Here are 8 goals to consider attaining before you're 18.

1. Make a long-term financial investment in the stock market.

2. Read the Bible through entirely.

3. Hold down one job for at least 6 months—a year if possible.

4. Read Dale Carnegie's book, *How to Win Friends and Influence People.*

5. Obtain a basic idea of what career direction you are going to take, and make the necessary plans for school or training.

6. Develop one strong friendship that you will keep for life, no matter where you both end up.

7. Save enough money to buy a decent used car.

8. Keep your grades up, and get your high school diploma.

3 Problems of Those Who Don't Plan

Planning is one of the great secrets of success in any area of life. The great thing is this: The God we serve already knows how the future is going to look so He can help us plan better than anyone else. Sadly, there are people who try to "wing it" in life. Here are 3 problems awaiting those who fail to plan.

1. You are setting up a life system for failure. You've probably heard the old saying, "Those who fail to plan, plan to fail." A lack of planning is actually a game plan to lose in life. Unprepared people are always unsuccessful people.

2. You'll never inspire others to follow you. People are afraid to walk in the dark. Ultimately, you are going to want people to help you get where you want to go. When people fail to see a plan for where you are going to take them, they are most likely not going to sign up for the ride.

3. You'll give up more easily. A plan gives you the approval you need to reach your goals and a definite finish line. A visual finish line will help you give 100 percent towards getting to where you want to go.

4 Steps to a Plan That Works

The Bible tells us in Psalm 37:23 NKJV that the steps of the righteous are ordered of the Lord. A good plan isn't accomplished in just 1 or 2 huge leaps that get you there quickly. It is going to take time and it is going to take multiple steps. Here are 4 steps that are necessary for a successful plan.

1. Write down your goals. You cannot develop a plan when you haven't clearly established what you are trying to accomplish. It's got to be more than "I want a job." What kind of job do you want? What hours do you want to work? What kind of skills do you have? What work environment are you looking for? Be clear about your goals.

2. Consult with people who have been where you want to go. This may involve taking a person to lunch or visiting them at their workplace. Perhaps you'll have to read a book or attend a seminar. Get the information you can on their journey to achieve success.

3. Put together the resources to make your plan happen. It may mean saving money, buying a weight set to train so you will make the football or soccer team, or simply writing down each resource and tool you'll need and figuring out how you are going to get them and use them.

4. Be realistic on the time line. We often try to bring our grandest plans to pass too quickly. Give your plan the time it needs and don't quit until you get there.

6 Keys to Getting the Most Out of Your Time

Time is a commodity that can never be replaced. If you lose money or a possession, you can always get it back. But once you turn 16, you will never be 15 again! The Bible tells us to "redeem," or make the very most of, the time we have. (Eph. 5:16 NKJV.) Here's how:

1. Appreciate the value of your time. You only get 86,400 seconds a day. Use them well.

2. Set priorities. Remember these words from Zig Ziglar: "You can't do everything you want to do, but you can do anything you want to do."[3]

3. Plan your daily and weekly schedule. Write it down.

4. Don't allow unnecessary interruptions and time-wasters to steal valuable time from your projects.

5. Politely hang up on telemarketers!

6. Learn to delegate things that other people can and will do for you. You can't create more time, but you can use the time of others.

4 Ways to Discover What You Can Do

Proverbs 18:16 NKJV promises, "A man's gift makes room for him, and brings him before great men." Believe it or not, God has put special gifts of ability into your life. Here are 4 ways you can find out what they are.

1. Seek God in prayer, asking Him to reveal your abilities. Jeremiah 33:3 tells us when we call upon Him, He'll show us things to come.

2. Ask people close to you. Solicit the evaluation of friends, parents, teachers, coaches, and others you trust to give their observations on your gifting.

3. Go after things you have in your heart. Never be afraid to step out and attempt something you've never done.

4. Faithfully do the little things you are asked to do, the things you don't like as much. God promises to give you bigger things when you do the small stuff well. (Matt. 25:23.)

YOU'RE HIRED!

Imagine yourself on the set of a popular reality show. For days you've been pitted against other young business professionals, working relentlessly with your team to vie for a prestigious position with a well-known entrepreneur.

Now it's time to enter the boardroom and find out who will be staying for another week and which unlucky contestant will hear the dreaded words: "You're Fired!" Your palms are sweaty and your muscles tense, yet there is an undeniable excitement in the air as you step into the room with this larger-than-life icon of the business world and glance at the cameras taking your image to audiences nationwide.

Thinking back over the recent flurry of activity, your mind races with all the different working styles demonstrated by your teammates. Some worked with honesty, integrity, and diligence, while others spent their time complaining and causing strife. Some team members cooperated well together for a common goal while others were more cut-throat, doing and saying whatever it took to get ahead with no concern for those their actions might hurt. You wonder which qualities will be perceived as strengths in a future employee of the tycoon and which will be deemed weaknesses.

What does it really take to be successful in business, school, and life?

Now imagine yourself for a moment in a different kind of boardroom—the final meeting before the Master of all creation who will decide your fate for eternity. Again your nerves are high, yet you are in awe of the magnificent presence before whom you stand. This time, it's not a matter of whether you're hired or fired; your heart longs only to hear the glorious words: "Well done, good and faithful servant.... Come and share your master's happiness!" (Matt. 25:21).

The same principles that will help you succeed in life will also prepare you for all eternity. On the pages that follow, you'll find lists of qualities that not only will help you be a success in this life and in the career you pursue, but will also be pleasing to your ultimate Boss, the Lord of the universe, and will set you up for an eternity of unthinkable joy and fulfillment.

6 Steps to Finding Favor in the Workplace

God wants to help you succeed in all your work. Your success in your job and career will be a direct result of your ability to get along with people. One of the coolest things in the world is having a job you love and working with people you really like. Here are 6 steps to get you there.

1. Don't treat your boss one way and everyone else a different way. People will see your hypocrisy and resent you.

2. Never cheat your company or business by stealing. I'm not just talking about their products or supplies; this also includes their time. If you're constantly late to work, take long breaks, or leave early, it's like stealing money out of the cash register, because "Time is money."

3. Don't try to destroy someone at your work in order to get that person's position for yourself. It will eventually backfire, and you'll be out!

4. When someone else does a good job at your work, compliment the person personally and in front of your boss.

5. Never try to take authority or leadership that hasn't been given to you. Just do your job, and stay out of business that isn't yours.

6. Always give 100 percent. If you can give 110 percent, you were never giving 100 percent in the first place!

5 Ways to Get a Great Job

I've held a job since I was 12 years old. I've learned how to work hard and have never been fired. I've discovered that if you give your best, you will have the opportunity to eventually do work that you enjoy and get promoted into a really cool job. Here are 5 ways to land a great job or career.

1. Get out into the workplace and hunt your job down. Knock on doors, set up interviews, and learn to sell your desire and ability.

2. Be sure you have properly trained and prepared yourself for the job you really want. If it means attending college, find a way to go to college. Read, learn, intern, volunteer, and do whatever it takes to become the best in your field.

3. Start out in any company or organization being willing to do the small things that other "big shots" aren't willing to do. It will separate and distinguish you from the pack.

4. Set your sights high. Don't allow your own self-doubt or other people's lack of support stop you from going after your goals.

5. Pray and trust God to open up the doors supernaturally. He can, and He will. (Jer. 33:3.)

5 Qualities of a Valuable Employee

I currently have about 20 full-time employees and interns who serve under my direction and leadership. Each one of them is extremely important and valuable in contributing to our youth ministry. Here are the 5 qualities that make workers valuable.

1. Diligent. They give you 100 percent of their effort 100 percent of the time.

2. Smart. They think as they work, always coming up with better ways to get the job done more effectively.

3. Faithful. They will take just as much pride in and give as much attention to the small details of their work as they do big things.

4. Loyal. They speak well of you, fellow employees, and the organization to others and always seek what is best for the organization.

5. Productive. They get results, are careful with the finances, and help the organization grow.

7 Rewards of a Diligent Worker

Many people seek to do the least they possibly have to at a job. What they fail to understand is that they are blocking the blessings of God from coming their way. Proverbs 21:5 assures us that the plans of the diligent will lead to plenty, while those who are hasty in their work will find poverty. Here are 7 rewards of the diligent worker.

1. Promotion. Hard work will be rewarded with higher positions of responsibility.

2. Recognition. A diligent person will stand out from the crowd, acknowledged by many.

3. Wealth. Companies and organizations will pay good money to those who do their job well.

4. Respect. You will gain esteem from your friends, your family, your peers, and your community.

5. Opportunity. You will find yourself becoming very valuable to others who will open new doors for you to walk through.

6. Influence. You will earn the privilege of teaching, training, and mentoring those who will want to learn from your success.

7. Fulfillment. You'll never have to live with regrets, wondering what you could have accomplished if you had only given your best.

4 Kinds of People Who Constantly Get Fired

I have been in the workforce for more than 20 years and have never been fired from a job. Unfortunately, along the way, I have seen many others who worked alongside me suffer this difficult experience. Most of the time, they had no one but themselves to blame. Many of these people fall into one of the following 4 categories:

1. Those who cannot receive instruction or correction. Instead of acknowledging their shortcomings and making the appropriate changes, they overflow with pride and refuse to listen.

2. Those who cause strife in the team. They may be talented and diligent workers, but they allow jealousy, competitiveness, and hunger for power to sabotage their abilities.

3. Those who refuse to continue to grow and improve. These people accept mediocrity and will not pay the price to increase their knowledge and ability to perform at their highest level.

4. Those who are not truthful. No matter how talented a person is, the individual cannot help an organization if he or she cannot be trusted.

5 Things God Says About Work

Our work is very important to God. Unfortunately, there are a lot of teenagers who don't think seriously about work until they get out of high school or even college, but now is the time to develop good work habits in your life. A strong work ethic will virtually ensure success in any career you choose.

Here are 5 critical things God's Word has to say about work.

1. If you don't work, you won't eat. (2 Thess. 3:10.) Work is the exchange God has created for all of us to gain finances to provide for our daily needs. God didn't say to pray, hope, or beg—He said to work.

2. We are to work as if our bosses were Jesus—not human beings. (Eph. 6:5.) Even when the boss isn't looking, the Lord sees all that you do.

3. Our work should produce good fruit and results. (Col. 1:10.) Don't just put in the time, but learn how to get results.

4. If we're faithful and consistent in the small things in our jobs, we'll be promoted to bigger tasks and responsibilities. (Matt. 25:23.)

5. A worker is worthy of one's pay. (Matt. 10:10.) You should be paid fairly for your work; and once you've agreed on a wage, you have no right to complain about your pay. Be cheerful!

6 Keys to Being Promoted by Your Boss

No one likes to work at a job without being recognized and even promoted for one's labor. There are reasons why some people seem to climb the ladder of promotion and authority, while others remain on the lowest rung.

Here are 6 keys to your promotion at your work.

1. Always arrive a few minutes early for work and then stay at least a few minutes late.

2. Do not allow personal issues or other relationships at your job to take time or focus away from your work.

3. Never complain about your pay. You agreed to work for that amount, so be grateful!

4. Ask your boss from time to time if there is anything you can do to improve your performance.

5. Work with your head, not just your hands. Think of ways to do your job more effectively.

6. Don't continually badger your boss with requests for promotions or raises. Let your work do the talking, pray, and trust God; and when the timing is right, ask to speak to your boss, without being demanding.

3 Secrets to Real Success

There's not a person reading this book who doesn't want it—success. You don't want to go out and fail. Success is your goal, and God wants to help you attain it. But it is important to define real success so that you know exactly what you're praying for.

1. Real success is never compared to someone else's achievements. Your measuring stick for success in your life is not your big brother or best friend. Success for you is based on the talents God has given you and how well you apply them.

2. Real success is loving God and loving people. All the money, power, and recognition in the world will not satisfy the deepest yearnings of the human soul. That's why many of the unhappiest people in the world are rich athletes, entertainers, and entrepreneurs. In the process of reaching your goals, love God and love people.

3. Real success is long term, not short term. (Matt. 16:26.) If you succeed by the world's standards for 70 or 80 years but pass from this life into eternity without God, what have you gained? Don't lose your soul while trying to gain in this world.

3 Reasons It Is Cool To Make Good Money

In the past, some Christians have believed and taught that all Christians should be poor. Sadly, they have had a very poor understanding of what God says in the Bible. While the Lord is opposed to us making money our god and primary focus, He wants to bring finances into our hands for the right purposes. Check out 3 reasons why making good money is cool with Him.

1. God wants you to learn how to provide well for yourself and your family. In fact, He says that if you don't make money and provide for your home, you are worse than an infidel (a really bad sinner)! (1 Tim. 5:8.)

2. God wants you to use your money to sow into His kingdom in order to make provision to take the message of Christ around the world. It costs money to print Bibles, support missionaries, and build soul-winning churches. (2 Cor. 9:6-11.)

3. Simply, God loves His children. As a Father, He wants to meet all of our needs and even our desires. As long as we keep our eyes and hearts focused on Him, it is His will to bless us abundantly. (Ps. 37:4; Matt. 6:33; Phil. 4:19.)

3 Keys to Discovering Your Career

When you are young, your career is more of a dream than a reality. But before you know it, you're well on your way. There are thousands of possibilities for your future profession, but there's something specific that God has planned just for you. It's never too early to begin the process of finding the career that is best suited for you. Here are 3 keys to discovering your career.

1. Find out what you're good at doing. Some people are gifted artistically, some musically, some mechanically. Focus on the things that you do well, and begin to develop the skills that correlate. Your future career will likely come from something that you are naturally good at doing.

2. Try it on for size. Just because you're good at something doesn't mean you enjoy it. Your career will not last long if you don't enjoy what you are doing. See if you can do an internship in the career field you are interested in. Maybe you can get a part-time job during the summer.

3. Narrow down your options. Take a look at all of the possibilities. Rule out the career choices that you know would not bring you fulfillment and the one you try and dislike. The shorter your list, the more specific training you can seek.

Reality Check

6 Careers You Can Start in Your Teens

While your youth is a time to have fun and enjoy life, it is also a time to learn the value of work and ambition. The Bible has much to say about the importance of working diligently.

Here are 6 careers that you can embark on right now.

1. Newspaper business. Throw a paper route, and discover the satisfaction of getting a job done early in the day.

2. Investment broker. There are companies that will take investment capital of just $50. Learn how the market works, and start investing a little at a time.

3. Graphic arts. If you have a bent for drawing and art, offer your assistance to those in need now. I know 14- and 15-year-olds who design logos and Web sites for companies and churches.

4. Film and video production. With an inexpensive camera and some software, you can be in the "movie" biz. My son began to be paid for his projects when he was just 15 years old.

5. Lawn care. If you have a mower and a weed-eater, distribute fliers in your neighborhood and sign up accounts to cut and trim grass after school and all summer.

6. Child care. Make yourself available to families for quality baby-sitting services. Be a good one, because they are hard to come by!

3 Reasons to Quit Your Job

While I believe it is extremely important that you are steadfast and faithful in your work for an employer, there are times when you have very legitimate reasons to quit. Here are at least 3 of those reasons.

1. Your job requires you to compromise your Christian principles. If your work is causing your walk with God to be compromised or diminished, it is probably time to quit. Perhaps it requires you to constantly miss church. Maybe you're being asked to do something that goes directly against your beliefs and values. Trust God and He will lead you to something better.

2. Fellow employees are having a negative effect on your life. The Bible instructs us not to be unequally yoked with unbelievers. (2 Cor. 6:14.) If you are "yoked" together with unbelievers on your job who are causing you to compromise or suffer temptation that is bringing you down, it's time to change jobs. The Bible says that with temptation, God gives a way of escape. (1 Cor. 10:13.) It says to "escape," not stay there and try to overcome it.

3. The Lord is leading you to something better. There are times when you may have a good job that is meeting your needs, but God has been preparing you for the next step—something even better. When a season of faithfulness in one place comes to an end, be obedient to step out to His next assignment for your life.

4 Secrets to Make Work Go Fast

Isn't that the hard thing about a job—that it seems to take forever? How come when you do something you enjoy, like sports, shopping, or hanging with friends, time just flies, and when you have to work in the yard for 2 hours, time almost seems to go backwards! Help is on the way. Check out these secrets to move that second hand around like a sprinter.

1. Great mental preparation. Don't approach work with visions of how long and bad it's going to be. "I'm going to get this job done and have a good time doing it!" This is the kind of mentality that will speed everything up.

2. Slice your work up into smaller parts. Don't sit there thinking about everything at once. Concentrate on cutting the grass in the front yard first. Now attack the back yard. Then get the weed eater out. One part at a time and you won't feel overwhelmed.

3. Create personal competitions. Try to figure out an easier or better way to get a job done. How can you do it faster without sacrificing quality? When you create challenges for yourself, you tend to forget about the time.

4. Quit looking at your watch every 22 seconds!

5 Qualities of a Job Well Done

It's not enough just to do a job. It's important that you do it well. In the work world, when you don't do a job well, you get to do it again, which takes even longer. Or you get fired. This, by the way, is not good. So you might as well figure out how to do work that makes people happy.

1. Do all you do with joy. Be happy, or at least force a smile on your face and fake it!

2. Start strong. Get started on time, and do the hardest stuff first while you have an abundance of energy.

3. On each part of the job, ask yourself, "Is this the best I can do, or am I trying to get by with as little as possible?" You know what the answer should be.

4. Always look to add a little extra. It may take 5 or 10 extra minutes, but do more than you were asked to do. "Oh yeah, Mom, I took out the trash too" are beautiful words to hear.

5. Finish what you start. Do a thorough check. *Is everything done? Did I put my tools away?* A job well done is a job that is complete.

4 Ways to Get Hard Work Done More Quickly

Very few of us actually enjoy hard work. That's why it's called "hard work"—because it's hard. The harder the job, the more likely people are to put it off. The longer it is put off, the harder it usually becomes to complete. Just because it's hard doesn't mean that it is not worth doing or worth doing well. Here are 4 ways to get the hard work done more quickly.

1. Break down the job into steps. Making the big job into several smaller jobs will help you see the progress along the way. Breaking it down will also help you decide how long it will take and what you will need to accomplish the task. Taking a small amount of time at the front will save you time in the long run.

2. Start right away. Procrastination only makes the work much more agonizing once you start. Don't let yourself think about how much you dislike the task, or what you would rather be doing. Just start somewhere; you can't finish something that you never begin.

3. Find out if there is a better way. Don't just search for a faster way to work; look for the best way. Doing things the right way will always save you time. Cutting corners may seem to help speed things up, but you don't have to redo something that was done correctly the first time. It is always a good idea to look for the latest and smartest ways to do a job. Sometimes there may be a better tool or technique that could help you finish faster and end up doing a better job too.

4. Recruit help when appropriate. If a job is your responsibility, or if you are expected to complete the work, do it yourself. If you can have help and the help is available, use it. Don't be so proud that you waste time on something that could have been done in half the time if you would have let others help.

3 Reasons "Working Hard" Levels the Playing Field

There is no substitute for hard work. Working hard will open doors of opportunity that would not have been available otherwise. The greatest achievements do not always belong to those who have the highest score, but to the people who are willing to work hard to accomplish great dreams. Those who are busy working will quickly surpass those who have a head start financially or socially but refuse to combine hard work with lofty ambition. These are 3 reasons why "working hard" levels the playing field.

1. Talent cannot work hard. Talent will take you far, but many talented people have failed because they didn't work. Working hard can help make up for a lack of talent and put you in a position to succeed. Even if you are the most talented person in your field of choice, if you sit still you will get passed by someone who is hustling to make things happen. Talent is like a seed; if it is not active, it cannot grow.

2. You can't steer a parked car. If you try to turn left in a car that is parked, you won't get very far. In order to make choices and navigate through life, you need to be moving. Working hard, no matter where you are, ensures that you are in motion and able to choose the right path. (Prov. 12:24.)

3. Hard work makes up for your background. No matter where you came from or what kind of family you have, if you are diligent you will be successful. People want to be surrounded by those who are passionate and will work hard to make each

endeavor a success. Others will go out of their way to involve you, if you make the choice to be faithful and industrious. Your willingness to work hard and finish a job will be far more attractive than your family name.

4 Bible Verses to Help You Work Better

God's Word has much to say about the way we go about our work. There is a right way and a wrong way to do everything, including the labor of our hands. Here are 4 critical thoughts to remember when we put our hands to a task.

1. Our work is ultimately for Jesus Christ, not man. The Word of God says in Ephesians 6:5 that even when our natural boss isn't looking, the Lord sees and inspects all that we do.

2. Our work must be planned out well. Proverbs 21:5 says the plans of the diligent make you rich, not just being diligent. So make sure you are working smart, using wisdom to get your job done in the most efficient way.

3. Our work should produce results. It's not just about producing a few beads of sweat. Make sure you are accomplishing something in what you do. Colossians 1:10 tells us to be fruitful in every good work.

4. If we don't work, we won't eat. (2 Thess. 3:10.) Work is an exchange of your valuable time for your bosses', customers', or clients' valuable money. The old saying, "There's no free lunch," is true. Life is an exchange every day. What you put out determines what will come back.

IS FEAR A FACTOR?

A reality show that's had astonishing success is all about fear. On each episode, a different set of contestants compete against one another to see who will be the most courageous in facing and overcoming some of their worst fears. The competitions range from daring to outright disgusting. In one contest, participants may be asked to walk on a moving plank suspended hundreds of feet in the air while trying to collect a certain number of flags. Another contest might involve getting into a tank filled with dozens of venomous snakes. The show has become perhaps most well-known for its eating contests. To pass to the next level, participants have to eat something incredibly foul, like a sausage filled with roaches or leeches. To celebrate the show's one-hundredth episode, the host served up a hearty helping of rat stew.

Fear and caution are sometimes confused. Exercising a certain amount of caution is a good thing. God equipped us with the ability to recognize danger so we can avoid it. For example, we have a natural aversion to eating certain animals because of their lack of cleanliness. While the creatures served on the show are examined carefully to make sure they aren't diseased, a person wouldn't last very long in the real world on such a diet without contracting some deadly disease. Likewise, a healthy respect for the law of gravity keeps us from jumping off of a twenty-foot cliff expecting to land on our feet unharmed.

However, fear can become overpowering and keep us from doing what we know we should do. A fear of failure might keep a person from trying out for the team or applying for that dream job. A fear of intimacy might cause a person to end a potentially wonderful relationship before it's had a chance to blossom. Whatever the situation, we should use wisdom, but we should never allow fear to control us or fuel our actions.

So how do we deal with our fears when they threaten to get the better of us? Some people in the Bible had a pretty good idea. Many of them faced challenges that make the reality show competitions look like child's play. Daniel spent the night in a den of lions—and lived to tell about it. Shadrach, Meshach, and Abednego had a prayer meeting in a fiery furnace—and weren't even singed. Jesus faced the worst kind of death at the hands of Roman soldiers—and by doing so triumphed over death and the grave. What was their secret? They all must have felt the effects of fear. In fact, the Bible says that Jesus was in such inner turmoil as He faced the cross that His sweat was like blood (see Luke 22:44). Yet each of these men had faith that their God was bigger than their situations and could carry them through any challenge as long as they placed their trust in Him.

Don't allow your fears to hold you back from the wonderful future God has planned for you. Instead, let Him know about your fears; then allow Him to turn those fears into lion-taming, fireproofing, death-defying faith.

4 Fears You Must Conquer Every Day

Fear is the primary tactic of your enemy, the devil. All through the Bible, we are told to "fear not." Fear will immobilize you and stop you from reaching your goals and full potential. You conquer your fears by studying, speaking, and acting on the Bible, God's Word. When you do, you will conquer these 4 kinds of fear every day.

1. Fear of failure. This lie tells you God is not strong enough to help you succeed, and it is perhaps the greatest attack of fear.

2. Fear of the future. This lie compels you to believe God is unable to see what lies ahead for you and to direct you in every step.

3. Fear of the past. This haunting deception says that because of where you or your family has come from, God is unable to make everything good today. (2. Cor. 5:17.)

4. Fear of comparison. This lie tries to talk you into believing God favors someone else more because that person appears to be doing better than you. The enemy wants you to believe God has given up on you.

3 Keys to Motivating Yourself to Do Difficult Things

The easy things come easy, don't they? It's easy to be motivated to play our favorite sport, shop at our favorite store, or eat our favorite dessert. But how do we motivate ourselves to do the hard things like the day-to-day work at school or home, regular exercise, eating right, or any activity that you know you should do, but everything inside of you says "No"? Here are 3 keys I've picked up along the way to motivate myself.

1. Just start. There is something magical about forcing yourself to "turn the ignition key" and get things going. It will give you that little bit of momentum to get rolling in the right direction. Make yourself start!

2. Keep the end result in mind. The Bible says in Proverbs 29:18 (KJV), "Where there is no vision, the people perish." If you don't remind yourself why you're working, exercising, praying, reading, etc., it will become too easy to quit. Motivate yourself with a vision of what this activity is going to accomplish.

3. Reward yourself. Create some kind of reward that you are going to give yourself for completing this task or activity. If might be watching your favorite show, getting a smoothie, taking a nap, or something else you like to do. God rewards us for doing right, so why not reward yourself!

4 Obstacles That Come With Every Great Opportunity

Great opportunities do not come without challenges. Often, the greater the opportunity, the greater the challenge will become. If it were always easy, people would be walking into something new all the time, and you would never hear anyone complain about never getting a break. Preparing now to meet those challenges will keep you from being surprised and give you courage to overcome each one. Here are 4 of the biggest obstacles that come with every opportunity.

1. Sacrifice. If people did only the same things that have always been done, we would still be living in caves and using leaves for clothes. Great advancements come when someone is willing to sacrifice, because they are passionate about what was possible. Whether it is time, energy, money, fame, or popularity, as you set your priorities you will have to sacrifice certain things to make the most out of any great opportunity.

2. Knowledge. Many times the full potential of an opportunity is never realized because the people involved simply didn't know enough. That fact has kept many people from trying to accomplish great things. As you undertake any great opportunity, there will be times when you feel like you just don't know enough, but that doesn't mean that you are not the right person for the job. Make the choice now to study and surround yourself with wise people and you will succeed where others have failed, even if you don't always immediately know the answer.

3. Distraction. There is so much going on in the world and so many things that try to grab your attention. If you don't choose to stay focused, you will get tripped up by one of the biggest obstacles to opportunity. Those who can maintain their focus and see vision through to reality are the people who will be able to seize the opportunity and make the most of it.

4. Fear. The single biggest obstacle to success of any kind is fear. Fear will cause you to freeze and question if you really can do anything at all. Fear can make you say "what if" instead of "why not?" If you allow yourself to look at opportunity through eyes of fear, you will watch each opportunity pass you by and miss the great rewards of making a stand. God doesn't want you to react out of fear; He wants you to enjoy all the blessings of moving past that obstacle and making the most out of your opportunities. (2 Tim. 1:7.)

3 Reasons Your Thoughts Will Affect Your Performance

If you've ever been at a great height and had someone tell you, "Don't look down!" then you already understand this concept: You will focus on and be drawn towards what you allow to dominate your thoughts. These are 3 reasons your thoughts will affect your performance.

1. Your thoughts before a competition establish your image of the event, your team, and your performance. By focusing your thoughts on the game plan, you begin the process of winning before you ever step onto the field.

2. Your thoughts will determine your level of success in difficult circumstances. If you let fear or anxiety dominate your thoughts, you move the game from the playing surface into your mind by allowing fear of failure to make you freeze or keep you from trying again after a mistake.

3. A disciplined mind allows you to move past distractions and focus on the task at hand. It is difficult to win in sports, so thinking about the way someone is officiating the event or who is watching can make an uphill climb even harder.

Reality Check

3 Thoughts You Must Keep Out

If your thoughts affect your focus and your focus determines your direction, then here are 3 thoughts that you must keep out so you can keep moving in the right direction.

1. "What if I fail?" Don't spend your time thinking about failure; think about what it takes to win. Allowing yourself to think about failure makes the event more about how you will look or whom you will let down rather than being about the competition itself.

2. "What do others think about me?" Fans and spectators will always have contrasting opinions. But, good or bad, the opinions of other people cannot score points or win races. If you practice hard, keep your character strong, and always give your best effort, the results will speak for themselves.

3. "What about my past?" Whether you have missed your mark 1 time or 100 times, dwelling on that will only keep you from reaching it again. Replace those thoughts by thinking about how good it will be to succeed or setting a personal reward for each achievement.

EXTREME GIVING

There is one reality show that stands out from the rest because of its aim to produce joy, its happy endings, and, more than anything, its focus on giving. This Emmy award-winning show seeks out deserving families whose lives would be drastically improved by a home makeover. Each episode begins with a "Good Morning" greeting from the host as he informs the family that they have been selected for the show. A team of hundreds of skilled workers then swoops in on the house, giving of their time, energy, and amazing talents to transform the home into a fairy-tale dream.

Most of the families selected for the show are givers themselves who have been so focused on taking care of others that they haven't had the time or resources to improve their own homes. One episode focuses on a couple raising two children of their own and four foster children whom no one else wanted because of their troubled backgrounds. The family needs a bigger house so they can take in still more troubled foster children and give them the chance to be a part of a real family.

Another episode is about an army medic who lost his right leg when a roadside bomb struck his convoy in Iraq. The family's house is too small and narrow to properly accommodate an amputee, and they need a renovation to make the house more suitable for the master sergeant's new needs. Still, these obstacles haven't stopped the sergeant from continuing to serve the army as an instructor or his wife from studying to become a counselor for the families of soldiers who have been injured or killed.

If the families aren't enough to inspire viewers, the show's multitalented cast certainly will. Judging from each of their long lists of past accomplishments, it's doubtful whether any one of the show's creative team members really needs to be working. They could be relaxing at home, enjoying the rewards of a successful career. But instead, they've chosen to go on the road—repeatedly facing tight seven-day deadlines to accomplish what would normally take at least four months and giving up time with their own families—so they can be the first to see the grateful smiles on the faces of families who have been handed new hope for the future.

No matter what your talents or how successful you are at your chosen career, your greatest rewards in life will come from what you give away.

4 Reasons You'll Have More by Giving Away

Of course, we know that the Bible tells us to give a tithe (one-tenth) of our income to our local church, and offerings after the tithe to worthy causes. (Mal. 3:10-11.) There are at least 4 reasons you'll have more after you give.

1. The Bible teaches that giving is like planting a seed. Every seed produces a huge multiplication of its kind. (2 Cor 9:10.)

2. God promises to open heaven's windows and pour out blessings that you cannot possibly contain. (Mal. 3:10.)

3. Other people are naturally (and supernaturally) compelled to bless those who are unselfish in their giving. (Luke 6:38.)

4. Giving puts your faith into action, and faith is always rewarded abundantly by God. (Heb. 11:6.)

3 Reasons You Should Tithe

There are really more than 3 reasons you should tithe; but if these don't inspire you to tithe, another 100 reasons won't either.

1. God says if you don't, you're robbing Him. (Mal. 3:8.) This doesn't sound like a very good plan. I'm sure God has a good security system that lets Him know anytime a thief robs Him of His tithes. Do you think God is going to bless a thief who is robbing Him?

2. God said that if you do what He says, He will flood you with blessings. It sounds like a good thing to be flooded with blessings. Get your boat ready for God's good flood.

3. God will work His pest control on anything that will try to attack your finances. Some people lose great financial crops because of pests, accidents, theft, and so forth. Use pest control by tithing.

God says, "Test me in this" (Mal. 3:10). Put Him to the test. Honor Him with your tithes, and watch the blessings flow your way.

7 Rewards of the Giver

If you think you get the short end of the deal by being a giver, think again. Take a look at these 7 rewards Scripture promises to those who give.

1. You will prosper. (Prov. 11:25.) That's much better than the alternative.

2. You will be refreshed and encouraged by other people. (Prov. 11:25.) We all need this at different points in our lives.

3. You will get back what you give, but it will come back bigger and better. (Luke 6:38.)

4. God personally sees to it that you receive your reward. (Eph. 6:8.)

5. You will be flooded with good things. (Mal. 3:10.)

6. You will have supernatural protection over your finances. (Mal. 3:11.)

7. You will have treasure in heaven that no one can take away. (Luke 18:22.)

Take advantage of the rewards available to you by being a giver. You can watch others be blessed, or you can obey God's Word and receive blessings too.

3 Reasons God Wants You to Be a Channel

Webster's Dictionary defines a *channel* as "the course that anything moves through or past."[4] If you are willing to become a channel, God will be able to trust you with wealth and possessions. Too many Christians become wells instead of channels, holding on to what they get, refusing to allow their blessings to flow to others. So here are 3 reasons God is looking for you to be His channel.

1. As a channel for blessings, you will reflect God's character. God's very essence is to give. John 3:16 says that He so loved that He gave. When you give is when you are most like God.

2. As a channel, you will see no limit to what God can bring your way. When the Lord knows He can trust you to obey Him with all your provision, you are unlimited in your potential.

3. A channel is always left with the residue of whatever comes through it. Even as you obey God in giving, He will see that you continue to be blessed in the process.

3 Keys That Will Open the Windows of Heaven

In the Old Testament book of Malachi, God makes a promise to all His children. When we obey Him in the giving of our income, He will open the windows of heaven and pour out such blessings that there will not be room enough to receive them. (Mal. 3:8-12.) That means you will always have more than you need so that you can pass on your blessings to others as well. Here are 3 keys to getting those windows open in your life.

1. Bring in your tithes and offerings consistently. Your tithe is one-tenth of your income or paycheck from where you work. Your offering is over and above the 10 percent that is given in some way to extend God's kingdom.

2. He says to put your tithe and offerings into the storehouse so there will be food in His house. God's house today is His church. Your tithe belongs to your local church that you attend. Your offering can go to any gospel-preaching church or ministry that you see bearing good fruit.

3. He tells you to prove Him with your obedience. To prove Him means to put Him to the test, expecting Him to come through. This simply means to use your faith when you give, believing that He will meet your needs and desires.

7 Promises Guaranteed to Every Giver

When you obey God in the giving of your finances, you step into a special part of God's covenant with you. Giving consistently moves you into a new realm of supernatural provision. Here are 7 promises that will be yours if you give.

1. There is a harvest on the way back for every financial seed you plant. (2 Cor. 9:10.)

2. All of your needs will be met. (Phil. 4:19.)

3. You will have an abundance to give even more in the future. (2 Cor. 9:7-8.)

4. The devourer (Satan) will be rebuked over your life and possessions by God Himself. (Mal. 3:11.)

5. Spiritual fruit (souls of men and women) will abound to your heavenly bank account, which means you will reap extra rewards in eternity. (Phil. 4:17.)

6. You will receive back in direct proportion to the generosity of your gift. (2 Cor. 9:6.)

7. People who associate with you will have a supernatural, God-given desire to want to bless and assist you in every way. (Luke 6:38.)

5 Ways You Can Give Without Using Money

While giving in other ways will never replace God's instructions to give financially, there are other very practical, tangible ways we can give. So keep giving in your finances, but start thinking of other ways to give of yourself as well. Here are some ideas to get you started.

1. Serve in your local church. You may be a greeter, usher, or prayer worker, but do something.

2. Look for opportunities to help people in your daily life. It may be assisting someone whose car has broken down on the side of the road or helping up a child who has fallen. Look for ways to be a blessing.

3. Offer to serve at a mission for the poor during the holidays, such as Thanksgiving and Christmas.

4. Take a week's vacation or part of your summer vacation and go on a mission trip.

5. Write a letter or make a telephone call to someone who has made an investment in your life. Let the person know how much you love and appreciate him or her.

3 Kinds of Giving Every Person Ought to Do

One of the unbreakable laws of the universe is the law of sowing and reaping, seedtime and harvest. (Gen. 8:22.) It usually doesn't feel like it at the time, but when you give your money into the ground of good works, it will produce and come back to you multiplied many times over. Here are 3 kinds of "money seed" you should sow, expecting God to bring a harvest back to you.

1. Sow the tithe into your local church. A tithe is one-tenth of what you earn, and we are commanded in Scripture to give into the "storehouse," or where we receive our primary spiritual food—our church. (Mal. 3:10.)

2. Sow special offerings or gifts into ministries that are reaching people and to other worthy causes that are truly impacting people. (Phil. 4:15-19.)

3. Sow into the lives of those who are poor and unable to provide for themselves. (Prov. 22:9.) Keep your gift as private as possible so as not to humiliate the one who receives it.

3 Reasons Givers Find Unusual Favor

Favor can bring you before the right people and set up the right circumstances. Wouldn't you like to have favor? As a giver, you can. Here's why:

1. It's a spiritual law. As you give, it is as if you are making deposits into a favor bank account that you can withdraw from at any time. (Luke 6:38.)

2. People like givers. As you give, you become a giant magnet for unusual favor. Don't you enjoy being around givers? I thought so.

3. God is on your side. As you are obedient to God's Word, God will open up doors of favor in your life.

5 Scriptures That Focus on Giving

Every day you will have a choice whether to give or not to give. Whether your little brother wants to borrow something or a crazy friend wants you to shave his back hair, here for your encouragement are 5 Scriptures on giving.

1. Luke 6:38: Giving not only blesses the receiver, but also the giver.

2. Proverbs 21:26: As the righteousness of God, we are not to be stingy in our giving.

3. 2 Corinthians 9:7: Be sure your heart is in the right place while giving.

4. Matthew 10:8: God has blessed us so that we may bless others.

5. Acts 20:35: The giver is better off than the one who receives.

WILL YOU ACCEPT THIS ROSE?

How will you know if you've found true love? Maybe you believe in love at first sight or in just letting fate take its course and lead you to the love of your life. Or maybe you have a well-thought-out list of your ideals and expectations for your future spouse.

One reality show attempts to help a lucky bachelor find the love of his life. From thousands of applicants, the list is narrowed to twenty-five eligible bachelorettes for the bachelor to choose from. In order to make his decision, the bachelor is whisked through a series of individual and group dates with the ladies to help him determine whom he might fall in love with. On each episode, the bachelor is supplied with several roses to hand out to the ladies he'd like to get to know better. Those who receive a rose get to stick around for the next episode. Those without a rose at the end of the show have to say good-bye to the bachelor and their dreams of finding love on national television.

While the participants usually claim that the show's method of finding love works, viewers are left wondering how two people could really find true love in the midst of all the drama. With all the fighting, deception, and back-stabbing that inevitably occurs when twenty-five women compete for the affection of one man and the short time in which participants are given to get to know each other, one must wonder how the difference between love and infatuation could possibly be recognized under such circumstances.

While recognizing true love can seem confusing at times, God has given us some great guidelines to go by. They're listed in 1 Corinthians 13:4-7: "Love is patient, love is kind. It does not envy, it does not boast, it is not proud. It is not rude, it is not self-seeking, it is not easily angered, it keeps no record of wrongs. Love does not delight in evil but rejoices with the truth. It always protects, always trusts, always hopes, always perseveres." Look for these qualities as you search for the love of your life, and work on loving in this manner.

Attraction and shared interests are important to consider as well, but a relationship based on God's kind of love will stand the test of time and will endure through all kinds of hardships. And you'll be surprised at what things can become interesting to you because they're important to the one you genuinely love.

As you search for the love of your life, incorporate 1 Corinthians 13 into your thoughts and actions so you'll be able to recognize true love when it comes your way.

3 Reasons Friendship Is More Important Than Romance

Romance is a good thing. As a married man, I know. However, friendship is more important: It should be the foundation that romance is built on. Let's take a look at 3 reasons friendship is more important than romance.

1. Longevity. Friendship is long lasting. Romance is temporary. Romance is defined as a strong, usually short-lived, attachment or feeling. Friendship is there for the long haul.

2. More than a feeling. It's a fact. The feeling of romance will come and go. Romance has a lot to do with its environment and circumstances. Friendship, on the other hand, is there whether we feel it or not.

3. You can be yourself. You don't have to worry about impressing others. There is no need for you to present yourself in an unrealistic manner to gain affection. A true friend will still love you when you've had one too many Big Macs.

Reality Check

3 Things Love Is Not

Many times, people misunderstand what true love is all about. It is quite common for people to assume that love is some icky-sweet emotion we feel and has nothing to do with intellect or common sense. Psalm 85:10 says that mercy and truth meet together. Truth, honesty, and standards must always be applied in showing God's love to others. God loves us, but He also requires us to respond to Him appropriately. Here are 3 things that love is not.

1. Love is not a doormat. Love is never a license for people in your life to use or abuse you in any way. Jesus always stood up to abusive people like the Pharisees.

2. Love is not sexual. In fact, if you really love someone, you will not have sex before marriage. Sex in marriage is simply a physical expression of love that already exists in the hearts of two people who have committed their lives to one another forever.

3. Love is not an emotion. Just because you don't "feel" God's love one day doesn't mean He has stopped loving you. I don't physically live with my parents anymore. But just because I don't feel their love each day doesn't mean they have stopped loving me. The Bible promises that God's love will never fail you. (1 Cor. 13:8.)

6 Attributes of Real Love

You can't buy love, and you can't replace love with money. What many people call love is really "lust." Read 1 Corinthians 13 to discover the true definition of love. Here is a quick summary of 6 attributes of real love.

1. Love gives with no strings attached. Some people give nice gifts but attach strings. Real love gives expecting nothing in return.

2. Love looks for what it can give rather than what it can get. This perspective would change 99 percent of American relationships. Do you see people as opportunities to gain something for yourself or as an opportunity to give?

3. Love is quick to forgive. It doesn't keep a running tab of past offenses. Freely God has forgiven us; freely we should forgive others. (Matt. 10:8.)

4. Love is patient. This is tough in today's "must-have-it-now," drive-up-window society. But love is patient with others because God is patient with us.

5. Love has a humble heart and attitude. Real love knows that anything good we have is because of God's goodness in our lives. We can't take the credit. It all belongs to God.

6. Love is respectful and courteous of others. Guys, this sounds like being a gentleman; and girls—before you "amen"—this sounds like being a lady, as well.

Reality Check

5 Signs a Relationship Is Centered on the Love of God

When you first meet someone you are attracted to, there is usually a warm fuzzy feeling inside. Your heart pounds and maybe you even get goose bumps, but these feelings shouldn't be confused for God's love. You may have a "crush" or "puppy love." However, God's love is much deeper and more sincere. Here are 5 signs to tell if you are in God's love.

1. You love the other person for who he or she is rather than what you get from the person. God freely gave us His Son with no strings attached. (John 3:16.)

2. You have Christ at the center of your relationship. (Matt. 6:33.) When Jesus is at the center of all you do, your conduct will never bring you shame or regret.

3. You are waiting until marriage for any physical relationship. Love is patient and willing to do what is right before God and best for the relationship. (1 Cor. 13:4.)

4. You respect the other person's feelings and wishes. Love never pushes someone to compromise what he or she believes is right. (1 Cor. 13:5.)

5. Love seeks to serve the other person rather than be served. (Phil. 2:3-4.)

Use these 5 benchmarks to measure your relationship to see whether it is built on God's love or human lust.

OH, THE DRAMA!

A TV network with a large teen following has recently introduced a slightly different type of reality show, set up to feel
more like a prime-time drama than a reality show. It is based
on the real-life drama in the lives of a group of teenagers
growing up in California. These teens have everything—they
spend their days on the beach, drive fancy cars, and can fly
to visit friends or go to amazing spring break destinations at
the drop of a hat. Yet, they never seem to be happy. Their
dating sagas keep them in almost constant turmoil. When
they're not arguing with a girlfriend or boyfriend or stressing
out about someone not being interested in them—or someone
else being too interested in them— the girls are fighting
with the other girls over a guy and vice versa. A girl might
kiss a guy, then wonder why he acts like he has feelings for
her, or a guy might work his charm on a girl—maybe the
third he's dated that week—then wonder why she doesn't
want to be exclusive.

While it makes for some entertaining television, are these
the kinds of memories you'd really like to have of your high

school days? Is it really worth wasting all that time and energy on something you're not sure you want in the first place? Is dating worth losing friendships over?

Dating has its place. It can be a way to find out the type of person you'd like to marry and to learn how to relate to people of the opposite sex. But if you're not ready to enter into a committed relationship, dating can become an invitation for trouble and heartache for yourself and the person you date. Dating just for fun rarely seems to accomplish its intended purpose. Often one person takes the relationship more seriously than the other and gets hurt as a result. Sometimes love is expressed physically without any emotional attachment to back it up, leaving behind feelings of regret and emptiness. And even worse, spending all your time worrying about dating or the lack of it robs you of moments when you could be creating great memories or pursuing your dreams.

The great thing about your high school and college years is that there will be plenty of opportunities for you to hang out with both guys and girls in groups, without the added pressure of dating. If you can keep your relationships with the opposite sex at the friendship level for now, you'll avoid much of the drama and heartache that comes with dating before you're ready.

Don't let your life become material for a prime-time drama. Instead, focus your attention on friendships and opportunities that will last past high school, into your happy ever after.

Reality Check

3 Steps to Finding Favor With the Opposite Sex

There is something that happens when you move into your teenage years. All of a sudden, you're not as concerned about "girls' germs" or "boys' germs" as you were when you were 7 or 8. During your teens, God slowly prepares you to someday enter into the covenant of marriage. It is important that you learn how to properly treat and respect the opposite sex, since you will probably live with one of them forever. Here are 3 simple steps to remember.

1. Learn how to pass on sincere compliments about their character and accomplishments. Make them feel appreciated for who they are and what they've worked hard to achieve.

2. Be nice to all. Don't become "a snob" or "stuck up" because you associate only with those who are good-looking or popular. Remember, Jesus died and shed His blood for every person, not just the ones He liked.

3. Show respect and purity physically. Your body belongs to you. Other people's bodies belong to them. The only time this changes is when 2 people are married. So, until that time comes for you, stay clear of tempting situations. (1 Cor. 7:1-4.)

3 Things Dating Is Not

Dating is not really a biblical word at all. That doesn't mean it's wrong to go out with someone on a "date." But it is important to remember what the Bible has to say about developing romantic friendships. If you begin dating without some clear guidelines and boundaries, you are headed for disaster.

Let's start by taking a quick glance at what dating is not.

1. Dating is not for those who aren't ready. In my opinion, dating shouldn't even be a consideration until a young person is at least 16 years old. That's been "the law" with my 3 teenage boys, and they're doing just fine with it. That doesn't mean you can't have good friendships with the opposite sex; just keep things in a group environment.

2. Dating is not a great way to "really get to know someone." Why? Because everyone is on his or her best behavior during a date. If you really want to get to know someone, watch the person at school every day, or both of you get a job together at McDonald's. Eight straight hours over a hot greaser full of fries will tell you the real tale.

3. Dating is not all it's cracked up to be. Think about 2 people out together who hardly know each other. They're young and have limited social skills. They have to try to create awkward conversation for hours on end. The point is, it's usually a whole lot easier to get to know someone among a group of other friends who can help fill those awkward moments, keeping things fun.

Reality Check

3 Ways Christian Dating Is Different

The world's idea of dating is dangerous at best. That's why the Scripture tells us not to be conformed to this world, but to be transformed by the renewing of our minds. (Rom. 12:2.) We renew our minds with the knowledge of God's Word.

Here are 3 ways a Christian dating experience should be different from one in the world.

1. In the world, people date to check someone out; a Christian date is focused on building someone up. Dating in the world is like "trying someone on" like a pair of shoes—if they don't fit quite right for you, just disregard them and move on to someone else. A Christian's focus should be on encouraging each other in life and in one another's walk with God.

2. The world bases a large part of success in their dates on connecting physically, while Christians should be prizing spiritual things first. It's not that you shouldn't be attracted to someone by looks, but maintaining sexual purity must be at the top of your commitment to each other.

3. The world will often lie and deceive to achieve their goals in dating. Christians are to be committed to integrity and honesty. Don't try to be someone you are not. Tell the truth. If someone doesn't like the "real you," don't worry about it. Obviously, that person isn't "the one."

4 Signs That You May Not Be Ready to Date

Okay, you are at a new stage in your life. You have this attraction to the opposite sex that just wasn't there when you were 7 years old and still playing on the swing set in the back yard. Just because you have this new desire for romance doesn't mean it's time to date. Navigating through the complicated world of boy-girl relationships is like learning to fly a 747 jet. You need lots of instruction, preparation, and maturity before you try to take off.

Here are 4 signs that you may want to wait awhile before you get your engines going.

1. Your parents feel you are too young. Unless you are out of the house, 27 years old, and have a mom and dad who just can't let go, listen to them. They have been down the road you're on.

2. You have a significant problem with lust. If you are struggling with pornography and lack control in your thought life, conquer these areas first. (2 Tim. 2:22.)

3. God is not first in your life and priorities. A strong commitment to Christ is the foundation for any good relationship.

4. You believe dating will finally make you happy and fulfilled. People are not your answer. If you look to them for your hope and fulfillment, they can quickly become another one of your problems. Only Jesus Christ can fill you with a love that will take away that empty void.

Reality Check

4 Reasons Not to Try Too Hard

There are times when you can try too hard to get something you really want. I have seen this more often in relationships than in any other area. We must learn to be patient for God's plan for our lives to develop in His timetable, not ours.

Here are 4 reasons not to try too hard to find the one you're looking for.

1. Trying too hard and pushing too fast will result in a relationship with the wrong person. Often, if you're trying too hard, you take the first person who comes along.

2. Others will perceive you as desperate. This will naturally repel people, and you may miss God's best.

3. Trying too hard shows a lack of faith in God. Hebrews 11:6 says that we can't please God without faith and faith believes God will reward those who diligently seek Him. Don't seek after relationships. Seek God, and the right relationships will come.

4. You can go broke. If you become a "serial dater," you're going to take a major hit in your wallet, especially if you're a guy. This may be a bit on the practical side, but it's still true.

6 Reasons to Break Up With Someone

I discourage you from "going out" or "dating" too early. The Bible has much to say about developing good friendships but nothing about dating. As you grow older and a good friendship develops into a romantic relationship, be careful to keep things on the right track.

In case you're not sure, here are 6 reasons to break off a relationship that has gotten off track.

1. If you are being pressured in any way to take the relationship to a "physical" level, know it is inappropriate.

2. If you are verbally, mentally, or physically abused in any way, get out of the relationship—quickly.

3. If your partner doesn't show the spiritual drive and Christian attributes that you know are necessary to be strong for Christ, it's time to let go.

4. If you feel used in any way for what you have, give, own, or provide, don't stay in the relationship. Be sure the person likes (or loves) you. Period.

5. If you find the person to be a liar, don't stick around. Trust can be built only on truth.

6. If the person breaks up with you, let go. Seriously. There are many fish in the sea, and you may have just gotten rid of "Jaws," so move on!

3 Uncommon Things Every Girl Wants in a Guy

King Solomon said that a good man is 1 in 1,000 and a good woman is nearly impossible to find. (Eccl. 7:28.) So guys, if you want to be that 1 in 1,000, you can separate yourself from the pack by living up to these 3 uncommon characteristics.

1. A spirit of desire. Proverbs 21:25 says that the desire of a lazy man kills him. Girls are looking for young men who have vision, drive, and desire for life, and are willing to work to reach their goals.

2. A spirit of kindness. Proverbs 19:22 tells us that kindness is what is desired in a good man. Learn proper etiquette and manners in the way you should treat people.

3. A spirit of justice. A just person is someone who has learned to distinguish right from wrong and is not afraid to stand up for truth. Don't back down to the pressure of friends to do wrong or compromise. Have some backbone and be counted.

3 Uncommon Things
Every Guy Wants in a Girl

All right, ladies, turnabout is fair play. You have some expectations too. In a world that has become increasingly corrupt and vulgar, you can stand above the crowd by the way you choose to live. Anyone can follow the masses, but it will be the few who do the right thing who are exalted, promoted, and blessed with the best relationships and a bright future.

What does a real man want in a girl?

1. Devotion. A real man will chase a girl who chases after God and is unwilling to compromise and give in to the world. Be devoted to Christ and devoted to His plans for your life. Guys will follow!

2. Wisdom. Knowledge is the acquiring of facts and information. Wisdom knows what direction to go with those facts and information. Guys search for a young woman who has the ability to discern and make good decisions.

3. Encouragement. Throughout the Bible, we are instructed to encourage one another, inspiring others with our words and good works. Learn to build people up, not tear them down. A man needs a woman who believes in him and will be a regular source of strength and encouragement.

DON'T EVEN GO THERE

One reality show that aired over the summer surprised contestants with the news that the sleeping arrangements would be one guy and one girl per room. Other reality shows press contestants to give in to sexual temptation by setting them up on Jacuzzi dates or sending them on weekend excursions. There's even one show that's dedicated entirely to subjecting contestants to sexual temptation to see if they will give in, potentially ruining their real-life relationships.

Over and over, we see lives destroyed and relationships torn apart by sexual impurity and unfaithfulness. So why even go there? Satan knows that sex is one of the easiest ways he can distract us from God's plan for our lives. Taking a relationship to a physical level before marriage has the potential of causing a person to drop out of school because of an unplanned pregnancy. It can lead a person to become consumed with a relationship that lacks real potential and can draw him or her away from interests and activities he or she had previously been passionate about. Many bad marriages are entered into because of a false sense of intimacy rather than genuine love.

Hollywood often glamorizes sex before marriage, even making it seem like the responsible thing to do is to live together before committing to marriage. For some, sex has become just a normal part of the dating process, a way to supposedly get to know another person. Don't buy into this lie. Once sex enters the relationship, it's easy to substitute open communication with physical interaction. Time that would have been spent getting to know each other better is then wasted on engaging in an artificial sense of intimacy.

When sex is treated casually, it loses the beauty God intended it to have. God created sex to be the purest expression of love and intimacy between a man and woman who are truly meant to be together, who share a special bond formed by knowing the details of each other's hopes and dreams and having the same vision of a life serving God as one. God created sex for our pleasure, and He intends for us to enjoy it within the confines of marriage, without the guilt or bad memories of past physical relationships.

If you've already been involved in a physical relationship, it's not too late. You can start practicing sexual purity from this point on and still avoid many of the pitfalls that come with premarital sex. Otherwise, take the advice of the young newlywed in Song of Solomon 2:7 and "Do not arouse or awaken love until it so desires." The reward will be well worth the wait.

Reality Check

6 Reasons to Say No to Premarital Sex

The Bible teaches us in 1 Corinthians 6:18 to flee sexual immorality. God is not a "Grinch" trying to steal all the fun out of your teenage years. He wants to protect you and prepare you for a wonderful marriage relationship where sexuality will have its perfect place.

Here are 6 reasons to say no until then.

1. You will close the door on sin and its destructive nature.

2. The thought of raising a baby while you're a teenager will never enter your mind.

3. You will never have a doctor tell you that you've contracted a sexually transmitted disease.

4. Friends and classmates will never see compromise in your life that will cause them to talk behind your back and lose respect for who you are.

5. God will be able to trust you with His very best as you give Him your very best.

6. You will never have to deal with "ghosts of relationships past" in your marriage relationship.

7 Ways to Avoid Premarital Sex

It's one thing to know that we should flee sexual immorality, but you may be wondering, *How do I do it?* Here are 7 ways that you can avoid the sin that can destroy you and your future.

1. Sexual sin starts in the mind, so win the war there first by studying the Bible. Fill your mind with God's Word.

2. Stay in church. The more you hear the Word and stay close to other Christians, the better you will keep your focus on spiritual things.

3. Don't ever go out alone with a person you know will tempt you or easily give in to sexual sin.

4. Don't allow yourself to be alone with the opposite sex in a place where temptation is easily fostered.

5. Stay away from sexually suggestive books, magazines, photos, or Web sites that will stir up sexual desires.

6. Build relationships of accountability with parents and strong Christian friends. When going through a trying time, let them know and ask for their help.

7. Make up your mind. Never retreat. Let every new friend you meet know you are committed to sexual purity.

5 Steps to Overcoming Tough Temptations

As you grow in your relationship with God, you will find that there are things that still cause you to be tempted. Even though you are forgiven and walking in relationship with God, these temptations may still be very strong. Here are 5 steps to overcoming even the toughest temptations.

1. Avoid situations that tempt you. (Gen. 39:10-11; 2 Tim. 2:22.) One of the best ways to avoid sin is to avoid the situations that you know are a temptation to you. Each person is different, and each person may struggle in different areas after they are born again. But by being humble enough to admit that you are tempted in a certain situation and avoiding that area, you will save yourself heartache down the road.

2. Keep God's Word in your heart and in your mouth. (Ps. 119:11.) By keeping yourself full of God's Word, you automatically reduce your ability to be tempted. (Gal. 5:16.) If you focus on God's promises and His love for you, the payoff for giving in to any temptation seems insignificant.

3. Choose ahead of time to make the right decisions. By making the tough choices before you face the temptation, you allow yourself to make decisions in a neutral environment without the heat of emotions. You will always make better decisions if you base them on your integrity. (Prov. 11:3.)

4. Be careful what you allow to influence you. (Prov. 4:23.) If you hang around the wrong places or the wrong people for long enough, absolutes can become blurred. By choosing wisely

who and what you allow to influence you, you guard yourself from temptation.

5. Look to God. It is always better to avoid temptation altogether when possible. But if you do find yourself in a situation where you are tempted to compromise, remember that God has a way out. (1 Cor. 10:13.) If you do the things that you can to avoid temptation, God will be faithful to help you right where you are in your moment of temptation.

3 Important Steps to Take If You've Sinned Sexually

If you have sinned sexually, it's important to realize that God isn't mad at you. Read the story in John 8:1-11 about how Jesus responded to the woman caught in adultery. He didn't condemn her. He forgave her and told her to go and sin no more. Don't be afraid to go to God like Adam and Eve, who hid from Him in the Garden. (Gen. 3:8.)

Here are 3 steps to help you get back on your feet if you have sinned sexually.

1. Repent. (1 John 1:9 AMP.) This means to do a 180-degree turn from the direction you were going. Notice, this verse says He will forgive and cleanse you.

2. Reject condemnation from the devil. The Holy Spirit never condemns; He only convicts. Condemnation is a feeling of hopelessness. Conviction is a stirring to repent and move forward in God. (Rom. 8:1-4.)

3. Restore yourself spiritually by seeking godly counsel. Find a spiritual leader in your life, such as a parent, youth pastor, or youth leader you can confide in and receive godly counsel and encouragement from. (James 5:16; Prov. 28:13.)

Put these steps into practice, and you will be on course to recovery and to even greater spiritual heights than before.

4 Signs a Relationship Is Lust-Centered

Here are some signs you can look for in your relationships to see if you have strayed from God's kind of love to fleshly lust.

1. You look lustfully at the opposite sex. (Matt. 5:28.) This doesn't mean you can't look at the opposite sex in a decent manner. It's what you are thinking about as you do. If you couldn't look at the opposite sex, you would have to walk with your head down the rest of your life.

2. You're willing to compromise eternal rewards for short-term pleasure. (Heb. 12:16.) Take the path Moses did. He forsook the sinful pleasures of Egypt for the eternal reward from God. (Heb. 11:24-25.) The pleasure of sin lasts only for a season, but the reward of purity lasts forever.

3. You manipulate others to get what you want. "Baby, if you really loved me, you would prove it." If you really loved the person you said that to, you wouldn't ask him or her to compromise God's Word. The proof of love isn't physical; it's obeying God's Word and keeping Him at the center of your relationships.

4. You feel like you have to give in to the other person's pressure because you are afraid he or she won't love you if you don't. Perfect love casts out all fear. (1 John 4:18.) If your love is based on God's Word, you won't fear a human being. You will be more concerned about what God thinks than what anybody else thinks.

If you examine yourself against this checklist and find you are in lust instead of love, follow these steps.

1.   Repent. (1 John 1:9.)

2.   Renew your mind. (Rom. 12:2.)

3.   Rebuild your relationship on God's Word.

4 Ways to Avoid Sexual Temptation

You have probably seen someone mess up and make the excuse "the devil made me do it." This isn't a scriptural statement, because the devil can't make you do anything. He can only tempt you to sin. (Matt. 4:3.) You have to make the choice. Here are 4 choices you must make to help you avoid sexual temptation.

1. Avoid the places of temptation. (Rom. 13:14; 2 Tim. 2:22.) If you are around friends who feed you temptation, get new friends. If certain movies arouse temptation, change what you watch. Don't be alone with the opposite sex where you could be tempted. Stay in public.

2. Purpose to remain pure. (Dan. 1:8.) Daniel decided before temptation came that he would obey God's Word. You must decide up front to live pure. If you wait until you are in the middle of temptation, your resolve to do right will be weak.

3. Hold yourself accountable to someone. (Heb. 10:25.) Find a good spiritual friend who will encourage you in the things of God. When you know you have to answer to someone about your actions, it helps you stay on course.

4. Be full of God's Word. (Ps. 119:11.) God's Word is your weapon to overcome temptation. Willpower alone isn't enough. Jesus used Scriptures to overcome temptation. (Matt. 4:1-11.) If you put God's Word in your heart before the battle, it will come out in the battle when you need it.

You can overcome sexual temptation if you carefully and diligently follow these practical steps.

5 Reasons to Maintain Sexual Purity Before Marriage

The Bible instructs us to live a life free from sexual immorality. (Eph. 5:3; Col. 3:5; 1 Thess. 4:3.) However, God isn't trying to rob you of fun and pleasure. He has your best interest at heart. In fact, God created sex for our enjoyment as long as it is in the boundaries of marriage. (Heb. 13:4.)

Here are some of the reasons God instructed us to remain sexually pure before marriage.

1. God protects us from a broken heart. When you give yourself to someone sexually, you are giving that person your heart as well. If this person is not your spouse, then part of your emotions are in the hands of someone else. (1 Cor. 6:16.)

2. God protects you from sexually transmitted disease and possible premature death. (Rom. 1:27.) Every day young people die from AIDS. Not any of them ever thought it would happen to them.

3. God protects your marriage from emotional baggage from the past. You can be married to your spouse and have no guilt from past mistakes.

4. God also helps you protect your self-esteem.

5. You are worth the wait. If someone says he or she loves you but won't wait until marriage to have sex, then that person is lying. Love is patient. (1 Cor. 13:4.) You are worth waiting for.

Resist the temptation to give in to sexual pressure. God has your best in mind.

Reality Check

BEFORE "I DO"

One reality show takes two wives with extremely different views of how to keep a house and raise a family and has them swap homes and families for two weeks. For the first week, each wife must live by a set of rules that the other wife leaves behind regarding how her household should be run. During the second week, each wife is free to run the household as she sees fit. Watching these wives adjust to their new surroundings can be quite entertaining.

On one episode, a woman who was accustomed to cleaning her house every day was placed in a home where the family kept a goat indoors, along with several dogs and various other pets. She and the goat had to learn to get along for that first week, until she was allowed to make a nice home for it and its other four-legged friends in the back yard.

There are many adjustments to be made, but by the end of each episode, all of the husbands and wives involved usually find many qualities to be thankful for about each other and discover areas in which they can improve themselves and thereby improve their marriage. The show's format also creates a forum for open communication for the couples, an element that seems to have been greatly lacking for many of the participants on the show.

What do you need to know about the person you're thinking about marrying? Well, you may want to find out his or her stance on goats in the house for starters! Okay, maybe this isn't much of an issue for most couples, but being able to communicate your dreams and expectations for the future is an important part of preparing for marriage.

Get real with each other. Talk about the past. What has made you both who you are today? Talk about the present. What are each of your likes and dislikes, your values, your priorities? Talk about the future. What do you want in your career, your family, where you will live?

You likely won't agree on everything, and that's okay. But learning how to communicate your ideas and preferences with each other now will go a long way toward helping you work out differences in the future.

Reality Check

7 Areas of Preparation You Must Complete Before You Are Married

Here are 7 important, but often overlooked, areas to work on before marriage.

1. Spiritual stability. Make a strong spiritual foundation in your life. This foundation will hold your life together through all storms. (Matt. 7:24-27.)

2. Emotional health. If you have emotional areas that aren't healthy, such as unforgiveness, unresolved anger, and severe mood swings, take this time before marriage to fix these.

3. Physical fitness. This will help you attract the opposite sex. It's true your future spouse should like you for what's inside, but he or she will also have to live with what's outside. Take care of your body, and your body will take care of you.

4. Financial soundness. Develop good responsibility with your money. Tithe, give, and save. Guys, women are attracted to someone they feel will be a good provider; it helps them feel secure. Ladies, guys are frightened by reckless spenders; they are afraid they will never be able to satisfy your cravings for stuff. Be self-controlled and modest with your money.

5. Maturity. Be responsible in your actions. If you can't take care of yourself, how can you take care of a spouse and children?

6. Friendship skills. Learn to be a good friend. After all, marriage is spending the rest of your life with your best friend.

7. Solving conflict. Marriage will have conflicts and disagreements. The couples who last can solve differences with love and respect rather than sharp words and fighting.

Preparation time is never wasted time. The more you sweat in preparation, the less you bleed in battle.

6 Habits You Must Establish Now If You Hope to Enjoy a Happy Marriage

The habits you form today determine the kind of life you live tomorrow. Someone once said, "First form your habits; then your habits will form you." What do you want to be? Form the habits, and your habits will help you achieve your goal.

If you want to attract a great mate, form these important habits.

1. Patience. The ability to be patient with others' faults will reap you the fruit of great friendship. What you sow, you reap. (Gal. 6:7.)

2. Ability to listen. This is a very important skill. No one wants to hang around someone who monopolizes every conversation. Ask what others think, and listen to them.

3. Servanthood. Marriage is a commitment to give your life to serve another. Learn this now, and it will be much easier when you get married.

4. Humility. This is the ability to say, "I was wrong; I'm sorry." Many marriages end in divorce because someone could not admit fault or apologize.

5. Character. This is the ability to stick to your commitment even when you don't feel like it. There will be many days when you won't feel like remaining married to your spouse, but character will see you through it.

6. Love. Read 1 Corinthians 13 for a good description of what real love is. This is the glue that holds a marriage together.

Form these habits, and you will be destined for a rewarding and fulfilling marriage.

5 Signs That You May Be Ready to Marry

How do you know when you are ready to get married? By society's standards it is being eighteen, having money for a wedding ceremony, and a willing fiancé. However, there should be much more than these if you want a marriage that will last a lifetime. Here are 5 indicators that you might be ready for marriage.

1. You have a healthy self-esteem. The Bible says we are to love our neighbor as ourselves. (Matt. 22:39.) If we don't have a healthy love and respect for ourselves, how can we genuinely love others? After all, love is the foundation for a good marriage.

2. You are financially responsible. Learn to be good with your money. Arguments over money is one of the top causes of divorce. Don't spend every dime you make. Develop the discipline to save something each time you get paid—I suggest 10 percent.

3. You have developed a good friendship with your potential mate. Marriage is about spending the rest of your life with your best friend. Marriages that are built on physical or romantic whirlwinds usually don't last. Friendship is the foundation for a love that lasts forever.

4. You and your potential spouse are in agreement about your values, dreams, and goals. Too often people spend all their time planning their wedding and honeymoon and never

ask the real questions. Is this person I am about to marry going the same direction I am in life? Amos 3:3 NKJV asks the important question, "Can two walk together, unless they are agreed?"

5. You are prepared to live the rest of your life with this person just the way he or she is. Many people marry someone thinking they can change what they don't like about them after they get married. What if they never change? Can you live the rest of your life with their habits, quirks, and attitudes that drive you nuts? If they drive you nuts now, they will drive you insane later.

3 Things Marriage Will Do for You

Marriage is a wonderful thing. I have been happily married for almost twenty-five years to my wife, Cathy, and our marriage gets better every day. That isn't to say we haven't had our moments, but we work through them and our love and understanding for one another continues to grow. Here are 3 things that marriage has done for me and will also do for you.

1. Marriage gives you a great understanding of God's love. In fact, the Bible says that the Church is Christ's bride and He loved her and laid down His life for her. (Eph. 5:25.) One thing I have learned is that there isn't anything I wouldn't do to protect my wife from harm. The love I have for her would compel me to lay my life down for her if I needed to. This has really given me a clearer picture of how much God loves me.

2. Marriage teaches you how to love unconditionally. Many of today's marriages are ending in divorce because couples have grown tired of one another and they want something new and fresh. The wedding vows don't say "until I get tired of you" or "until someone better looking comes along." They say, "until death do us part." Marriage is about loving one another through the good times and the bad times. And the bad times can get pretty bad. But if you walk in unconditional love, the rewards of a great marriage will be worth it. Then the good times will far outweigh any of the bad ones.

3. Marriage teaches you to respect each other's differences. This is such an important skill to learn in life because there isn't

anyone else exactly like you. Marriage is about respecting and enjoying one another's differences rather than trying to mold them into your image. My wife's strengths balance my weaknesses and my strengths balance her weaknesses. Learning to enjoy the differences in one another will help make a life-long marriage great.

3 Things Marriage Won't Do for You

Since we were little children we've watched the movies about the fairy-tale marriage where the prince and princess ride off into the sunset and live happily ever after. Marriage is made to look like the solution to all life's problems. Few people ever stop to think about what marriage will not and cannot do for them. It is important that you don't enter into this life commitment with unrealistic expectations that cannot be fulfilled through marriage. This will lead only to frustration and disillusionment.

Here are 3 things marriage will not do for you.

1. Remove sexual temptation from your life. We live in a sex-saturated society. It's all over the TV, billboards, and movies—it's everywhere. Even in marriage you will have to keep your thoughts submitted to the Word of God regarding sex. Adultery happens in many marriages because someone doesn't keep their sex drive under the control of God's Word. David said, "Your word I have hidden in my heart, that I might not sin against You" (Ps. 119:11 NKJV).

2. Eliminate loneliness. God is the only One who can truly fill the relationship hole in your heart. When we learn to be satisfied by His presence, then we will truly be able to enjoy the company of others.

3. Fix all your problems. Many people think that marriage is the cure for all their problems. However, the opposite is true. If

you are not able to handle the problems you have now, you aren't ready for marriage. Marriage is the merging together of your problems with your spouse's problems. Thus, you have more problems. That isn't bad because you now have both of you to work on them; however, you must be ready for this new pressure. The bottom line is that marriage can be great, but it isn't the solution to all your problems.

Realizing the things marriage cannot do and putting your trust in God to make up the difference is a great step towards living the "happily ever after" dream.

4 Habits of a Happy Marriage

Habits make us what we are. If we form good habits we will have good success. But if we develop poor habits we will suffer the consequences. Winners form winning habits just as losers form losing habits. Here are 4 habits of winning marriages.

1. Never stop dating your spouse. When people are dating they can hardly wait until the next time they can go out with each other. From the time the date is over they are planning their next date. It consumes their thoughts. In happy marriages, couples never stop dating. They make it a regular part of their lives.

2. Keep doing the little things. Before marriage we work hard and are creative at winning the affection of the one we love—notes, flowers, candies, poems, and so on. But after marriage many people feel that they have won their prize and they can stop the pursuit. Never stop doing the things you did to win their affection. Keep doing the little things that say, "I love you."

3. Never go to bed mad at each other. Every marriage has moments of anger towards one another for various reasons. This is a part of relationships. The Bible warns us not to let the sun go down on our anger. (Eph. 4:26.) Often our natural reaction to arguments is to go to bed mad at each other and get even with the silent treatment. This only gives the devil a foothold in your marriage. (Eph. 4:27.) Work out your differences. Don't be too proud to say, "I was wrong. Please forgive me." It is better to be wrong and still

be married in your twilight years than to be right and die a lonely divorced person.

4. Faithful church attendance. The happiest marriages are the ones that build their life around God rather than trying to fit God into their life. If you try to fit God into your life, there will always be a reason you can't go to church this time, but you will next time. And so on and so on. Happy marriages put God and the church first.

Perfect Immunity

As one of the first reality TV shows to hit the airwaves demonstrated, winning immunity made the difference between winning and losing the game show. In the same way, in the real game of life, having immunity also makes all the difference in the end.

In the hit TV series, people scratch, claw, and cheat in order to win the coveted prize. In life's "game" you can strive and cheat and climb over people to be successful, but when your life ends, will that be enough to claim the prize? And what is the prize? The prize is the power of a life well lived here on earth, and the joy of heaven after death. The truth is that life continues even after you draw your last breath, and you definitely need immunity in order to end up on the winning side. For the winners, a home in Heaven with the One who created you and loves you most awaits.

Here is the challenge, however. You can't climb enough, strive enough, or do enough to claim immunity from sin—or find peace with God. According to life's handbook, the Bible, there is no winning of this immunity. And that is the kicker! You'll never be good enough and you can never do enough. God has a different set of rules than the ones on television. He says there is only one way to have this prize.

So, how do you get it? In the reality television show, the host always asks the contestant who wins immunity if he or she wants to give it to anyone else. No one ever does. But, in this life, Someone did just that for you. His name is Jesus. He lived a sinless life and therefore won perfect immunity. And here is the good part! When Jesus was asked if He would give it up, He said yes. He gave it up for you! He knew you could never earn it. So, He came here, lived a perfect life, and then sacrificed Himself on the cross in order to bear the judgment your sin deserved. Perfect immunity was the outcome. And now, Jesus offers to give it to you. All you have to do is say yes. You see, in the real game of life, you receive it as a gift. It is free to you, though it cost Jesus His life.

So, what will you do? Will you keep striving for immunity and end up getting voted out (of Heaven) in the end, or will you accept Jesus' love and gift to you, and live with God forever? You get to choose.

If you want to accept perfect immunity, pray this prayer from your heart.

Prayer for Perfect Immunity

My heavenly Father, thank You for Your love and for the free gift of eternal life and perfect immunity that Jesus won through His death, burial, and resurrection. I receive that gift right now, by putting my faith in Jesus. And I proclaim that He is my Lord and Savior forever. Thank You for forgiving me my sins. Please fill me with Your Holy Spirit and help me to live for You and tell others about Your gift of perfect immunity through Jesus.

If you prayed this prayer, you now have eternal immunity! You will be in Heaven with God forever. You are now a Christian.

In order to grow in your new life:

Tell someone about your decision.

Get a Bible and start reading in the book of John.

Talk to God about everything.

Find a Bible-believing church and attend regularly.

Endnotes

[1] *Matthew Henry's Commentary on the Whole Bible, Volume 1,* Hendrickson Publishers, s.v. "mighty."

[2] Maxwell, John. *The 21 Irrefutable Laws of Leadership.* Nashville: Thomas Nelson, 1998.

[3] Ziglar, Zig. *Top Performance—How to Develop Excellence in Yourself and Others,* Berkley Publishing Group, 1991.

[4] *Webster's New World College Dictionary, 3d Edition.* New York: MacMillan Company, s.v. "channel."

About the Author

Blaine Bartel founded Thrive Communications, an organization dedicated to serving those who shape the local church. He is also currently leading a new church launch in a growing area of north Dallas.

Bartel was the founding youth pastor and one of the key strategists in the creation of Oneighty, which has become one of the most emulated youth ministries in the past decade reaching 2,500 – 3,000 students weekly under his leadership. In a tribute to the long-term effects and influence of Blaine's leadership, hundreds of young people that grew up under his ministry are now serving in full-time ministry themselves.

A recognized authority on the topics of youth ministry and successful parenting, Bartel is a best-selling author with 12 books published in 4 languages, and is the creator of Thrive—one of the most listened to youth ministry development systems in the country, selling more than 100,000 audio tapes and CD's worldwide. He is one of the most sought after speakers in his field; more than one million people from over 40 countries have attended Blaine Bartel's live seminars or speaking engagements.

His work has been featured in major media including "The Washington Post," CBS' "The Early Show," "The 700 Club," *Seventeen* magazine, as well as newspapers, radio programs, and Internet media worldwide.

Bartel's commitment to creating an enduring legacy that will impact the world is surpassed only by his passion for family as a dedicated father of three children and a loving husband to his wife of more than 20 years, Cathy.

Take the Turn for God in Just 5 Minutes a Day

Witty, short, and inspiring devotions for teens from one of America's youth leadership specialists!

Teens can discover a real, action-packed, enthusiastic relationship with God. The thrive.teen.devotional is motivated by a very simple challenge: Give just five minutes a day to God and watch your life turn around.

At the end of eight weeks, the Word of God is going to be more real and alive to teens than ever before as they gain spiritual insights on issues like friendships, self-esteem, and prayer. The good news is that when one's mind is renewed, they experience a radical turnaround in every other area of their life, too.

thrive.teen.devotional
by Blaine Bartel
1-57794-777-0

www.harrisonhouse.com

Fast. Easy. Convenient!

- ◆ New Book Information
- ◆ Look Inside the Book
- ◆ Press Releases
- ◆ Bestsellers
- ◆ Free E-News
- ◆ Author Biographies

- ◆ Upcoming Books
- ◆ Share Your Testimony
- ◆ Online Product Availability
- ◆ Product Specials
- ◆ Order Online

For the latest in book news and author information, please visit us on the Web at www.harrisonhouse.com. Get up-to-date pictures and details on all our powerful and life-changing products. Sign up for our e-mail newsletter, *Friends of the House,* and receive free monthly information on our authors and products including testimonials, author announcements, and more!

Harrison House—
Books That Bring Hope, Books That Bring Change

The Harrison House Vision

Proclaiming the truth and the power

Of the Gospel of Jesus Christ

With excellence;

Challenging Christians to

Live victoriously,

Grow spiritually,